A PRIEST FOR ALL REASON

Father Faherty was born in St. Louis in 1914, entered the Jesuit Order at Florissant, Missouri, in 1931, and was ordained at St. Mary's, Kansas, in 1944.

A PRIEST
FOR ALL REASON:

WILLIAM B. FAHERTY
50 YEARS A JESUIT

ANGELA HARRIS

DICK FRIEDRICH

RiverCity
Publishers

Permission Acknowledgements

Courtesy of *Frontier Magazine:* "The Spirit that Built the West." Courtesy of *Missouri Life:* "St. Louis' Great 'New' Cathedral"; "Mr. Shaw's Garden." Courtesy of *The Southwest Courier:* "His Crucial Hour." Courtesy of *Colorado Wonderland:* "Easter Sunrise at the Ski Chapel." Courtesy of *St. Anthony Messenger:* "Beyond the Fog." Courtesy of *The Eastern Kansas Register:* "Jesuit Pioneers Set Pace for Kansas Church." Courtesy of *The Jesuit Bulletin:* "Father Van Quickenbourne: Religious Pioneer"; "The Mississippi River Valley and Westward Expansion"; "The Immaculata Chapel and the Big Fire"; "Peter Verhaegen—Pioneer Missouri Jesuit"; "I Was in Prison and You Visited Me"; "Father Claude H. Heithaus. S.J." Courtesy of *The Credit Union Bridge:* "One Man Point-Four." Courtesy of Piraeus Publishers: sections of *Wide River, Wide Land.* Courtesy of Academy Guild Press: sections of *A Wall for San Sebastian.* Courtesy of Newman Press: section from *Destiny of Modern Women.* Courtesy of Andrews and McMeel, Inc.: section from *Living Alone.* Courtesy of Continental Heritage Press: sections of *Saint Louis Portrait.*

Published by River City Publishers, Limited

Printed in the United States of America

Library of Congress Catalog Number: 81-52127

ISBN: 0-933150-27-X

Cover Designed by Sheila Harris

CONTENTS

This book is respectfully dedicated

to

Uncle Barby

our subject and inspiration

Chatting or preaching, the expression on Father Faherty's face shows his love for those in his congregation.

INTRODUCTION

The first time I met Father Faherty was frightening.

I was a beginning writer, he was an Editor of Queen's Work. He'd published (with kindly editing) a couple of my stories, and one day he called the army post where we lived and said he'd like to drop in and meet the family.

Little did he know: Besides five kids, we had two army chaplains -- Dominicans, who promptly demonstrated the marvelous intramural rivalry that bubbles merrily within the Church.

Not to worry, they said, they would entertain my august Jesuit visitor.

The entertainment they thought up was a ten-mile hike with a 300-foot cliff-scaling on the side. That would test civilian historian, editor, writer, theologian, BRAIN, (and what they didn't know, skier and tennis player).

Back from the hike, Father F was in great shape, so were the chaplains. I was exhausted. Groggy, I tried to look as if I were following the conversation. I picked up the cream and started to pour it into the sugar bowl.

The way they tell it, he looked alarmed; made a motion to stop me; withdrew the motion; apparently thought, "Maybe she intends to pour cream into the sugar bowl," shrugged, and relaxed.

Just the person to befriend a family like ours. Over the years, he became for all of us, priest, friend, confidant, balance wheel. We didn't see him much, but when we needed him, he was there.

1

A PRIEST FOR ALL REASON

Steve, home from the Army, used a <u>word</u>; I objected. Steve said, "Oh, Mother, don't be Medieval." Five minutes later, another <u>word</u>. At my protest, Steve laughed. "Don't be Victorian, Mother."

Father F murmured, "Congratulations, Tere. You just aged 500 years."

Now, our kids who live on the East Coast say, "Father F's coming, we'll be on the battlefields for a week." Exploring Bull Run, Gettysburg -- the whole Civil War, which he knows as if he lived it.

When our son Rocky was captured by the Viet Cong, my husband was in the hospital, the children scattered. Father asked me to write a booklet about Latin Americans. I muttered about people who expected me to write under such circumstances.

Unperturbed, he wrote a couple of questions. I answered them. His next letter asked a couple more. By the time he was through, I'd written the whole piece. He published it.

Father started the Writers' Sodality, in between counseling, seeing that confused people met whoever could straighten them out; at writers' conferences, he drew crowds, guiding beginners, putting his finger on the flaw for old pros.

Name it, he wrote it: novels, biographies, histories -- St. Louis, his love, lives in his writings.

"... the definitive ..." opens every review of his works.

Unobtrusively, in the form of friendship, he picks up all your scattered pieces, hands them back with a courtly savoir-faire that makes you think you did if yourself.

That's what Father Faherty did for one family, and we seldom saw him. Think about how many other lives he's reorganized with a word or a look, this priest for all reason.

All you have to do is look at him, and you've got a friend.

Tere Rios

* * *

"Balance Wheel." "Priest for all reason." Tere Rios' introduction puts high praise on this man. This book represents an effort (perhaps an arrogant one) at producing a definitive edition of William Barnaby Faherty by putting together selections, organizing his works. When we first confronted the task, it pleased and excited us. Then the pieces started to come in: first a couple of large cardboard cartons arrived. O. K. Next a folder of letters. A few days later, a box of articles. The following week, several manila envelopes stuffed with short fiction. Here a meditation, there a scholarly article. Now a book he had simply forgotten. The amount astonished us; we wished we had decided to put this book together to celebrate Father Faherty's twenty-fifth Jubilee rather than his fiftieth.

If the amount astonished us, however, the variety had us nearly paralized. Here we discovered a most amazing collection: advice for living, stories to entertain, prayers to comfort and inspire, essays to inform. All we had to do was to choose representative pieces to show the variety of subjects he writes about in the multiplicity of forms he writes in. Our first editorial decision came easily: we would hold our commentary to a minimum in order to allow his work to show as much of the man as possible.

The next decision had to do with organization. We decided on three sections. The first shows him in his three major roles (really overlapping roles as the reader will discover): historian, priest and writer. The second reflects what seems to us his major areas of interest: athletics, St. Louis, people, his church. The third section contains one piece, a chapter from what we consider his masterpiece: "The Fire That Seared the Spaceport" from Moonport, his history of the Apollo space program. Hoepfully we show the man through our selection of his work.

The man who emerges here is, most of all, a various man, a man of many interests and talents; a man both active and passive, who reflects both yin and yang: a historian who looks to the present, who brings the past to today: a devout worshipper who serves the world as a priest; a voracious reader who produces books; a sports fan who does not simply sit back at sports events but who has coached a variety of sports and played (still plays, in fact) a good many; a world traveller and citizen of many cities who shamelessly promotes his home town; a scholar who gathers information, a fiction writer who uses his information to make his fiction more true than life; detached and engaged; a lover of the underdogs, cool enough to portray them faithfully and warm enough to show his loyalty to them; and (perhaps his outstanding trait) one who can control numbers of facts, who can pull them into patterns, who can synthesize. He stands the only one (or at least one of the very, very few) to have written for both the <u>Catholic Encyclopedia</u> and the <u>New Catholic Encyclopedia</u>.

The next most prominent characteristic is his solidness, his calm. Barnaby Faherty believes: in the face of twentieth century life, he eschews the nihilism and its twin, cynicism, for a measured, stable and clear stance as a yea-sayer, to use Carlyle's category. He looks at life with the kind of scholarly integrity one expects from a Jesuit historian and does not flinch from the contradictions he sees. He accepts sympathetically the conflicts between what people ought to be and what they, in fact, are. This quality leads to passion and loveliness in the love of Hugh for the married Rosellen in <u>Wide River</u>, <u>Wide Land</u>. This feeling for others remains unmitigated, nevertheless, by any sentimentalist escape: Father Gibault instructs Hugh very firmly on the merits of such a liaison. Rarely does one find a writer (balance wheel) who tempers a steady commitment to principle with such humane instincts.

Instruct and delight. Wisdom and happiness. These ends, traditional in Western writing rarely co-exist in American literature today. Long missing from European letters, they have left American writing only in the past few decades. Today writing meant to instruct has very serious furrows on its brow. When we have lessons, it seems, we must also have high seriousness. And when we have entertainment, any purpose aside from pure escape will certainly draw critical fire. But a priest like Barnaby Faherty has centuries of perspective to engulf mere thirty-year-old fads. As a result we find in his work instruction that pleases and entertainment that teaches. The merging of these qualities makes his work nearly unique in the ninth decade of this century.

* * *

We wish to thank Linda Lashley for her patience and competence in preparing the manuscript as well as Edna Suerman for her aid on the design. Pete Genovese's contributions were many, varied, and valuable. Erby and Carol Young did not stint in helping at every turn -- from turn one right up to those frantic final moments that editors and writers always promise to avoid yet always find waiting for them. Their encouragement meant much to us; probably only their expertise mattered more.

Finally we must say that Father Faherty proved not merely helpful in compiling this volume, he worked with us all along the way. It goes without saying (and therefore probably needs saying) that all credit for the quality of the selections in the book rightfully goes to him. And, of course, responsibility for the selection, and thus for any favorite pieces missing from this book, rests entirely with us.

We hope readers will read for their pleasure and benefit what we consider to be the most representative selection of the quality work of Barnaby Faherty, a priest for all reason, as he celebrates his fifty years as a Jesuit.

Known around the country as St. Louis' historian, Barnaby Faherty stands in front of a sculptured scene depicting Father DeSmet blessing the Indians.

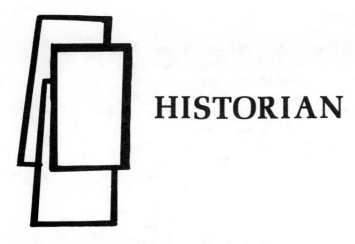

HISTORIAN

Current wisdom dooms those youth schooled
in narrow sectarian institutions to failure in
the secular world. Pity the poor boy educated
not just by nuns and priests in Catholic schools
from elementary school through graduate school,
but---worse yet---by Jesuits, an even more provincial element of the Catholic Church. This
wisdom collapses, however, when confronted with
the results of Barnaby Faherty's education. A
passion for painstakingly complete research, a
calm and reasonable perspective matched with a
dedication to God's justice: these qualities
do not mark the narrow-visioned intellectual
robot/pedant --- at worst stereotyped, at best
predicted by current educationists. Rather, in
fact, discussing these qualities as mere qualities does not ring accurate to one who knows
the man. These qualities, to a large extent,
mean Father Faherty; they constitute, for the
large number of his friends and acquaintances,
his person. The following chapter shows truly
catholic interests and vision in a man who has
lived fifty years a Jesuit.

Historians, of course, discover a history
by carefully researching facts: writers, on
the other hand, look for specifics and conflicts
to enliven their stories. Father Faherty's

dual background as historian/scholar and novel-
ist/ storyteller come together in the following
selections: the first selection not included
in the published version of Wide River, Wide
Land but included here; the second a portion of
a short story "North From Atlanta," followed by
two too brief parts from the published version
of Wide River. Here we witness history, that
is, we watch as though present, for he makes
history live. The confusion, the chaos of
battles from wars nearly a century apart come
alive with his scholar's eye, within his historian's perspective. He shows people living
and dying in battle--and we live history. We
experience the details which make up the stuff
of life: street names, freezing toes, the
shape of porches, the sounds of wind. But
while in these fictional pieces Father Faherty
uses history to make a good story, in "Father
Van Quickenbourne: Religious Pioneer," he re-
verses his fields, using his storytelling ability to make for fascinating history.

Make no mistake, however. This storyteller does not stand mired in the past; he
lives very much in today's world with his wide
range of interests in and commitments to, the
issues of the day. He does not see himself as
a mere reporter, nor does he, on the other
hand, shoot from the hip. His positions not
only arch clear, but they anchor themselves
firmly in hard research; his writing always
finds solid intellectual basis--whether expressed in a letter to the editor of a local
newspaper or in a book. The letter about desegregation published in the St. Louis Post
Dispatch reflects a scholar's reverence for the
truth, a dedication to historical, factual
accuracy; it also shows a person with a passion
for justice in matters of the moment. Another
current issue, feminism, received his attention
well before it became fashion among most of his
fellow historians. In the selection from
Destiny of Modern Women, Father Faherty uses
his considerable skills as a scholar as well as
his impressive ability to synthesize an ocean

of detail: the passage stands as a model of carefully selected information used to construct a solid and total picture.

"The Misssissippi River Valley and Westward Expansion" is a masterpiece of this synthesizing skill, this rare matching of abilities: the researcher who can put data into an accessible picture, the writer with a deep concern for thorough research housed in an intense interest in the movements of his culture.

The Lincoln Thanksgiving Day sermon and "The Spirit That Built the West" show him using this battery of abilities to become more than historian, more than writer, more than rhetorician: he adds his talent as a priest, as a preacher. He does not here simply search for truth to report; he does not just make the results of his study clear and interesting. He goes beyond even taking a position on a political issue. In this pair, one quite brief and religious, the other lengthier and more secular, he argues points. He counsels. He aims to move his audience. He shows himself: historian-writer-priest in action.

from Wide River, Wide Land.
previously unpublished section

"The Redcoats came marching on, with their heads high and the buttons on their uniforms glistening in the sunlight. I almost wanted to cheer. Instead I gripped my musket more tautly.

"Your father looked at me. It was my first battle. 'Good luck, Nick,' he said and punched me on the left shoulder.

"'I'll be all right, Brendan,' I said.

"Wait until the Redcoats march into the slaughter pen," Langlade had told us.

"That's just what it was to be. With flags flying, bagpipes playing, arms swinging in cadence, Braddock marched his Redcoats to their doom. The standard bearer passed by us, so close I felt I could reach out and tear the croix batarde from his hand. Then the bagpipers moved by. But still Langlade did not give the signal.

9

A PRIEST FOR ALL REASON

An arrogant cavalry officer rode up. Blond and red-faced, he looked at the small sassafras in front of me. He spat into its leaves. In that moment it seemed that all the Irish hatred of England, of green for red, of the men of Drogheda for Oliver Cromwell, coursed through your father's trigger finger.

"Wait, I said to myself. Wait, till Langlade --

"Then there was a shot. And the whole woods spat fire. The arrogant look of the British officer gave way to shocked surprise. A bullet hole appeared in his forehead. Blood trickled down his nose. He swayed crazily and fell.

"I saw smoke come from the muzzle of your father's gun. 'I got him, Nick,' he said more in wonder than in hate. 'I got him'.

"Men shouted in panic in the ravine. Triumphant war cries shook the wooded ridges. The red-coated column went down. As it did, men screamed and disappeared in the smoke. Horses milled about. The cannoneers could not wheel their pieces into position. Those at the far end of the line began to shoot in panic. The few gunners able to fire broke branches from the tops of the oaks. Over the smoke and panic, I could hear the voice of Braddock as he urged his men to stay in line, to form again into an ordered array as if they were on a parade ground.

"Caught in the whiplash of action in front of us, the Redcoats moved in a vast, confused jumble. Hopeless men groping about, not seeing an enemy but only spurts of gunflame out of thickets and ravines.

"Smoke filled the little valley. Men and horses lunged here and there in a tumult. As fires reached the dead bodies, I smelled the horrible odor of burning flesh -- the worst shock of the awful day! The slaughter went beyond belief.

"Farther down the line at the end of the ravine, a tall, square-shouldered, red-haired man in the uniform of the colonial militia put a little order in the group with him. He kept his men in battle array. But soon those at the front end of the line began to flee in terror. They threw disorder into the tall man's attempts to stand firm.

"The yells of the savages grew more terrible. Suddenly, the British fled in panic. The Indians rushed from their cover to finish the wounded.

"I picked up the saddlebag of the slain British of-

10

ficer. I thought at first I would also bring home a bag-pipe for you. But suddenly I had an urge to get away! To leave the place and try to blot out the picture. I spat an awful taste from my mouth. My stomach felt limp. I felt a sudden fatigue. We trudged slowly back to the fort, away from the slaughter of the Monongahela. We lay down at the foot of a black oak, but could not sleep.

"Braddock was a triple fool. When his men were going down in waves before us, he still insisted that they stand up in their bright red uniforms, in clear daylight, and face the fire they could not see. But I'll say this for him. He himself never hid. Three times horses went down under him. Each time he'd get up on another one. Finally he had to be carried from the field."

from "North From Atlanta"
previously unpublished

Sam Slug looked up at his brother's youthful face. The boy did not even need to shave regularly yet. Could anyone believe that he had seen his parents killed by Comanches, had fought all day at Shiloh, had stood his ground with Cleburne at Lookout Mountain, and then had rushed forward in those crazy attacks when Hood sent his outnumbered men to be slaughtered by Sherman's blue-coats in front of Atlanta? And still thought it was all fine, and the outnumbered, outgunned ghosts in gray were some-how going to win.

"We're right," Tommy said. "And they're wrong. Why don't they go back where they came from!"

"Houston freed Texas before you were born, Tommy," Sam said, "And brought her into the Union. Did you ever think that maybe Houston talked sense when he vetoed seccession?"

"Houston's an old man," Tommy said. "Things have changed."

Sam was sorry he had said anything. He had been trying for years to get a new idea into Tommy's head. Tommy caught on to other things so fast. But this--no! Tommy could march by a plantation and wave back at the owner and his family, and eat up that "heroic boys in gray" stuff, when actually he was to them just "white trash" who would never get through the front door. Tommy

could see the Governor of Georgia withdraw thousands of
men from the Army of the Tennessee in the face of Sherman's attack--because the Governor had other ideas on how
they might be used in defense of the state. Tommy would
think nothing of it.

Sam knew that ten-thousand uncomplicated fellows
like Tommy made the war drag on, and on, and on; made it
possible for butchers like Hood to throw men against
fences of fire...

The wintry road had been icy in the morning. But
now a weak December sun loosened the ground a bit. They
sloshed along, side by side. Sam felt better this way,
walking beside Tommy, thinking a lot, saying little. He
had ridden in command of the company for a time, while
Tommy walked. But that had been before the battle of
Franklin, the previous week.

"These shoes fit fine," Tommy said. "First dead
Yankee I found after Franklin. He must have just got
them new."

Sam looked at his own shoes. Tommy had scrounged
them, too. "I guess our shoes are the only good things
to come out of the battle of Franklin," Sam said.

"O no. I got this warm coat that night. Indiana
soldier. The blue color's a bit strong--but no bullet
holes in it. The fellow must have got clubbed to death."

Sam tightened his lips and said nothing. The only
way to quiet Tommy was to let him talk himself out.
Sometimes that was awful hard.

Sam buttoned the collar of his faded blue summer
jacket. He had picked it up in front of Atlanta. A
Michigan soldier simply figured he did not need it for
summer campaigning in Georgia. He didn't, and Sam didn't
then, either. He did now. It scarcely covered his thick
chest and short powerful arms. It was not much for a
cold December dawn, but better than most of the Rebs had.
He shivered a bit. He remembered with disgust that only
North Carolinians had worn new uniforms since 1862. All
the textile mills were in that state. Damn states rights,
anyway. Keep the uniforms for a time when the Tar Heels
would need them, and let the rest of the Army scrounge
clothing from dead Feds. Damn the whole business!...

Sam tried to think calmly about the battle of
Franklin. He couldn't. He could overlook his personal
grudges. What he could not overlook was Cleburne's death
in that mad attack. Cleburne and four other generals

12

dead in one senseless battle! Cleburne should have been commander, but Hood was. And he had sent his men against the Union trenches until they couldn't go any further. Cleburne had stayed in that wild tumult until he fell. Sam pulled the survivors back to safety.

Nonetheless, Hood had ordered his men to march on, over those mud-clogged, rainy, cold December roads of Tennessee. And towards what? Towards an army twice the size of the one he couldn't beat at Franklin. Towards an army entrenched on the hills of Nashville, poised, fresh, equipped, unbeatable, led by a man who never knew what defeat was.

Suddenly at twilight Sam and Tommy came over a ridge. They looked across the valley to the Capitol of Tennessee on the far crest, glowing in the last touches of a cold December sun.

"Pretty Capitol," Tommy said.

"Nicer than the one at Milledgeville," Sam admitted.

"It looks like an old hen gathering her chicks out of the cold!"

"It sure does," Sam said.

The building crowned the hill and seemed to embrace the houses of Nashville. Along the ridge the fires of the Army of the Cumberland stretched in endless line. Beaten at Chickamauga, that army had come back at Missionary Ridge. Somewhere on that ridge before them stood the indestructible Thomas, the Rock of Chickamauga.

Sam went through the motions of preparing for the night. They had little food. Only firewood was plentiful. The warm glow added a little cheer. Tommy was soon asleep. But Sam stretched on the ground, his head abutting the trunk of a white oak. The night was clear and cold. He slept little. He looked at the North Star directly above the capitol of Tennessee. One more day, he felt, and four years' work would be over. One more day and the endless walking, the dread, the shock, the bloody dying would be done.

But the next day Thomas waited. He didn't budge out of his line, waiting for the gray sheep to choose slaughter. It was almost as if Thomas was unwilling to have more men, Union men yes, but mainly Confederate, die in a battle without meaning. A battle could end only one way.

"If Hood had any courage," Sam thought, "he'd do the manly thing and hand over his sword. He knows what kind of man he faces. He faced him at Chickamauga, down in Georgia."

The thought of Chickamauga relaxed Sam a bit--the memory of that one glorious day of the Army of the Tennessee, but it was the man on the ridge to the north who had saved defeat from being disaster for the Feds. One man had stood firm against Longstreet when the men in gray thought they had a victory that would make the nation forget Vicksburg and Gettysburg, and the Union force fled almost in panic. One man had held his ground, and others joined him, and still others; and he rallied those broken bits of an army into a unified force, and preserved it intact in retreat until Grant and Sherman, relentless men, could come and set the Blue Army marching south again. That man was George Thomas, the Virginian, who had kept his soldier's oath to the Stars and Stripes.

But Hood did not intend to surrender. And Thomas did not move out of his entrenchments against the over-extended Confederate line. Neither the next day, nor the next week. Then came snow--the first many Southerners had ever seen--and ice. A fierce cold followed, but then damp, foggy, raw days came back. Two weeks dragged as the two armies waited.

Finally, in the raw pre-dawn on December 15th, shots came from the Confederate right. A little later, even more severe firing came from the left. The center of the line remained quiet. Sam could only surmise what had happened on the flanks. The late December sun came up, revealing a sad picture. Through much of the day, pressure drove the flanks back.

When darkness fell early, Hood pulled his entire line two miles to the rear in a shorter and stronger position.

Sam Slug rose stiff and hungry the next morning-- along with the rest of the Army of the Tennessee. Activity on the far ridge made him know that this would be the final reckoning. The winter sun came up late.

"We'll get them today," Tommy said.

"Yes, we'll get them," Sam answered. He wanted to say, "We'll get them in the center. We'll get them on the flanks. We'll get them in overwhelming numbers everywhere." But he didn't. He had one more job to do--to save Tommy one more day. He felt it had to be the last.

Suddenly the whole city of Nashville seemed to burst

out on them. In an endless attacking line, longer than
any Sam had ever seen, the Blue infantry moved relentlessly forward. On the hills behind the attackers the
big guns boomed. Never before had Sam had such a
sweeping view of a whole field of battle. He almost
wanted to shout in exaltation at the sight. Here was the
pageantry that made so many men--especially those who
have never been under fire--think of war as something
stirring and grand.

Rifle fire began to resound as the blue line came
into range. Some men went down, but others pushed by
them. Smoke began to fill the heavy December air. The
shouts of advancing men came through the smoke, then
the cries of the wounded and dying.

Sam felt the men around him tense. He looked
straight ahead. As last the infantry moved at them, no
longer a blue blur, but now individual men, farmers,
mechanics, hunters, store-keepers, who had to be stopped,
lest he and Tommy beside him, be killed.

Sam steeled himself for the onset. Rifle fire
stunned the blue line. It staggered a bit, reformed and
came on. Sam forgot the loaded revolver he carried under
his tunic. He fired his musket and, before he could re-
load, the two lines smashed together with fixed bayonets,
rifles used as clubs, fists.

At that moment Sam saw Tommy go down on his left.
He swung his body towards his brother to fend off the
onrush. A rifle butt crashed his head. Darkness...

He vaguely remembered seeing a few men walking
about in the twilight, and saying something he did not
really hear. Then blackness again. Finally he became
aware. He shivered. A dull pain clamped the entire
right side of his head. He touched his temple. No
blood. He sat up. His eyes were clearing now. Around
him, all was dark. But on the far ridge campfires
glowed. He could see the big dipper and the North Star
above them. Gradually he came to recognize the Tennessee
capitol. Time and place slowly came back.

He looked at the North Star a long time, recalling
what he could of the day. He remembered going to his
brother's aid, and the blow of the gun stock. Finally he
looked where he had to look--at the face of the dead man
to his left. But it wasn't the face of a man. It was
the face of a boy--his brother Tommy.

He wouldn't be able to find a shovel in the darkness. But he knew where they had dug a makeshift trench and erected a brestworks two days before. The dirt had been loose there. It would make a nice grave. He checked the place. It was as he had thought.

Instinctively he picked up his brother's body, slung it over his shoulder and carried it to the Confederate trench. He used his own gun stock as a shovel to cover the body with dirt, then stuck Tommy's musket in the ground beside the grave. He knew he still had his revolver; so he dropped his heavy musket.

He looked back at Nashville once again, then turned, and half-numb, walked down the road toward the south. The December night turned colder. He walked a long time. The stars moved far above him. At the edge of the clearing he spotted an abandoned farm house. He entered. The place was musty but warmer than the cold night. He flopped on an old bed and went to sleep.

from Wide River, Wide Land

As we passed Laclede's house, voyaguers carried pelts into the ground floor. "The basement serves as the warehouse," Nick said. "The family lives upstairs. Laclede plans to build a home in the next block north later on. We'll stop here a moment, then go over to see our old neighbor, Joseph Labusciere."

We left our gear at the warehouse and walked across the empty block to the west. "Here's where we'll build the church," Nick said. "That street is called Rue d'Eglise, the Street of the Church, and the next is Rue des Granges, the Street of the Barns." He pointed out a row of thatched-roof barns that stretched along the road.

We turned south on the Rue d'Eglise. I noticed that most of the houses were built of upright logs. All had large galeries, verandas that stretched along the entire front of the house and allowed a lot of outside living on rainy spring or fall days. Some had verandas on two or three sides. Laclede's headquarters alone, I noticed, had a galerie entirely around the house.

In Prairie du Rocher the pitch of the roof was the same over the dwelling and the porch. A few houses in Saint Louis followed this pattern, but more had a steep pitch over the dwelling and almost horizontal roof over the front and rear porches.

16

As we walked down the street, Uncle Nick could not
see over the palisades, but I was tall enough to see the
neat back yards. All had outside ovens; behind some
houses stood a little hut with an entire kitchen for
summertime use. Some habitants had already put in young
fruit trees on one side of the yard and a garden on the
other. All had an enclosed henhouse and some a small
stable for milk cows. Each house had its own well.

"If I build a house here," I said, "It will be out
where I can see the distant hills, watch the sun rise
over the river, and hear the mockingbirds -- but still
close enough to see my neighbors."

By this time we reached the house of Joseph
Labusciere. Our old neighbor from St. Philippe had come
out on the porch to greet us. "Bon jour, Nick, Bon jour,
Hugh."

"Bon jour, Joseph," we said in unison...

The snow caught us the fifth night after we left
Saint Joseph's. It came slowly in the twilight just
after we had made camp. The commander felt it would be a
long and fierce storm. He ordered us to gather several
days' supply of wood and to eat our first warm meal of
deer meat since we left the Fort. By darkness the wind
had risen and the snow flew through the air in frenzy,
pinning us at the foot of a ledge. I slept well that
night in spite of the blizzard that howled like some
giant wolf out of a prehistoric past. It still howled
when I awoke in the morning.

Even when the darkness gave way to a gray dawn, the
whirling snow blotted out the entire world. To venture
out would be senseless. We might have walked in circles;
and even if we went straight ahead, we would probably
have made only a few miles with a great waste of energy.
The commander wisely gave orders to stay where we were.

The day dragged on. Hour after hour. Minute after
minute. Unending. I thought of Rosellen and why I had
come. I lightly touched Rosellen's message through the
buckskin above my heart, and life and hope seemed to come
back to me. Finally night came once again. My arms
twitched, my knees and thighs quivered and jerked. My
eyes ached, but finally fatigue overwhelmed me.

When I awoke, the storm had ended, but the wind
still blew. Before us lay an endless expanse of white,
broken only by an occasional oak forest, and the rows of
trees that lined the river bank. We moved west along the

Illinois, trudging through the deep snow. No war parties would be out looking for us now--but that was small consolation. Cold day followed cold day. We reached the place where we had cached the canoes. Ice was so thick on the river, that the hopes of a swift canoe trip downstream disappeared in the snow-filled air. The supplies, however, were still intact. The guards were happy to see us back. We re-provisioned, cached our canoes in as safe a place as we could find, and trudged painfully along the banks of the Illinois.

My feet grew steadily colder as the skin of my moccasins grew thinner. Finally the right sole wore through. I cut a piece of leather from the fringe of my jacket. This makeshift patch gave slight protection. Every step became painful.

I could not think of the ten thousand steps I would have to take, but only of the next one--then the next. This was the only way to survive; to put one foot ahead of the other on the snowy ground; to lunge ahead, stumbling occasionally, but going on, not with any conscious effort, but mechanically, step after step, without thought or plan, fearing to think lest the reality overwhelm me; relentlessly on--freezing all night, even after choosing camp with care in the partial shelter of an oak forest; rising again, not because sleep had refreshed me, but because the sun was now overhead somewhere, hidden by the grey clouds; pushing on and on through country without hill or indulation, a flat bare table almost devoid of landmarks; on and on, down the endless river.

How I kept going I couldn't understand. I thought I knew the limit of my endurance, but I learned that there is almost no limit to endurance if the determination and motive are there. One week, two weeks, time was endless. Then one evening the sky cleared and the north wind died down. The stars stood out clear in a black, cold sky. The air grew colder and colder. No sleep came that night. It was too cold.

I felt better when the order came to march early the next morning. By ten, the sun warmed the clear air. The snow began to melt. We passed the ice-line on the Illinois. The river flowed free alongside us, restoring our spirits. We might have to move our legs mechanically ten thousand times more. Yet now we knew we would make it. In early March we were home.

"Father Van Quickenbourne:
Religious Pioneer"
from Jesuit Bulletin, October, 1965

The accomplishments of Charles Felix Van Quicken-bourne stand out clear in the annals of midwestern America. He was a successful preacher among the growing towns of Missouri and Illinois. He founded the Missouri Mission which eventually became a Jesuit province. He opened the novitiate at Florissant. He held together a dogged little band of Belgian novices to form one of the greatest Jesuit endeavors in the last two centuries. He acceded to Bishop Rosati's request for a group of men to staff Saint Louis College, soon to grow into Saint Louis University. He began the first Jesuit mission among the Indians of the western United States. Out of this devel-oped an extensive apostolate among the tribes of the Northwest. The editors of the Dictionary of American Biography justly included an account of his career among those who had made significant contributions to American life.

On this, the 150th anniversary of his entrance into the Jesuit order, a recounting of his career should prove profitable and interesting.

Charles Van Quickenbourne was born in Belgium one year before George Washington became president of the United States. He entered the local seminary and was ordained for the diocese of Ghent. He taught classical languages until such a time as the Napoleonic Wars forced the school to close. He then served for a time as a parish priest.

In 1815, the year of Napoleon's downfall, he joined the newly restored Society of Jesus. He wanted--ever since boyhood--to become a missionary among the Indians of North America. Assigned to the United States in 1817, he became master of novices at White Marsh in Maryland. Fr. Peter J. Timmermans served as his assistant, both on his home missionary ventures and as master of novices. The novices had come from Belgium at the challenge of the great missionary, Fr. Charles Nerinckx. All were to prove above-average men. Felix Verreydt, Judochus Van Assche, and John Baptist Smedts eventually became steady and effective missionary pastors. John Elet and Peter Verhaegen were to have noted careers as educators and administrators. Peter Jan De Smet was to gain world-wide fame as a missionary, a peacemaker between the government and the hostile Sioux, and a writer of fascinating accounts of the western country.

In 1823, the American Jesuit superior, Fr. Charles Neale, agreed to the request of Bishop William DuBourg of "Louisiana and the Floridas" to send a group of Jesuits to begin Indian missions in the Missouri Valley. Fr. Van Quickenborne and Fr. Timmermans came west, along with the six novices just mentioned, and a seventh, Francis de Mailliet. Three lay brothers accompanied them, Henry Rieselman, Peter DeMeyer, and Charles Strahan. Arriving at Florissant in June, 1823, they took up residence on the farm which the Bishop had provided. Living conditions at Florissant had all the hardships of early frontier days. Only the sacrificial kindness of Blessed Philippine Duchesne and the other Religious of the Sacred Heart at the convent in Florissant helped the group through the first long winter.

From the very onset of his efforts in Missouri, Van Quickenborne undertook too many things. His extensive activities amid unhappy personal relationships suggest that he was as changeable as the March weather. Actually he was consistent within his inconsistency. He simply did not stop to realize that he demanded of others things not required of himself.

Before he had seen the novitiate farm, he talked with the explorer General William Clark about opening an Indian school. Without adequate housing for his community, he invited Indian chiefs to send their sons for a Jesuit education. Within a month of arrival in Missouri, he dismissed, as unsuited for Jesuit life, Francis de Mailliet, a young Belgian who had left his native country, crossed the ocean, and traveled by flatboat down the Ohio. In a letter to his superior in Maryland, Van Quickenborne accused his only priest companion, Peter Joseph Timmermans, of serious dereliction of duties. Within a year he had to write in an entirely different vein to the superior. Young Fr. Timmermans had worked diligently among the people of Florissant and the vicinity. When he died in May, 1824, less than a year after his arrival, the outpouring of grief among the villagers was such that Van Quickenborne had to admit: "His death has produced here the effect which is ordinarily produced by the death of a saint."

Bishop DuBourg wrote to the Maryland superior asking him to send a superior for the organization of the Missouri Mission. The Bishop recalled that now only one priest of the Society was left; and he feared that he too would fall under the burden of increased work. After all, Van Quickenborne already acted as vice-superior, taught theology to the scholastics, missionized such neighboring settlements as Florissant and St. Charles, and was spiritual director of the Religious of the Sacred Heart.

Van Quickenborne should have allowed those young Jesuits who had already finished part of their theology course to complete it as quickly as possible. Bishop DuBourg and later Bishop Rosati urged this. Instead Van Quickenborne plunged precipitantly into plans for the Indian school. Within a year of the Jesuits' arrival at Florissant, two Sauk boys came. The next month two Iowas followed. St. Regis Indian Seminary opened.

While this venture seems quixotic, it did have the encouragement of General Clark, America's most knowledgeable man on Indian affairs, and the support of the prominent Secretary of War, John Calhoun. The United States Government granted a subsidy for the program. This fact must be admitted: the subsidy, along with the revenue from the Florissant farm, did help to support the infant Missouri Mission.

When Joseph Rosati became coadjutor to Bishop DuBourg in 1824, Van Quickenborne assumed the post of Vicar General of Upper Louisiana. Now at last he decided to do something about the seminary training at Florissant. Unfortunately, he did the less wise thing. Instead of advancing the better prepared men to ordination, he assigned John Elet and Peter Verhaegen to assist in teaching the other scholastics. When the health of Van Quickenborne finally gave way under the excessive strain of his many duties, the request for another priest from Maryland was answered. On October 10, 1825, the Belgian count, Fr. Theodore De Theux, and Brother John O'Connor arrived at Florissant.

Finally in early 1826, Van Quickenborne decided that two of the men should be ordained, Smedts and Verreydt. At the last minute, however, he substituted the name of Peter John Verhaegen for Felix Livy Verreydt. The two men travelled to the Vincentian seminary at St. Mary's of the Barrens near Perryville, in southeast Missouri, where they were ordained in late winter. During the following summer the new superior of Maryland, Fr. Frank Dzierozynski, paid a visit to Missouri. He insisted that the other scholastics be given their final examinations in theology. Less than two months later, on September 23, 1827, Bishop Rosati came to St. Ferdinand's Church in Florissant to ordain Elet, Van Assche, De Smet, and Verreydt.

The newly ordained priests began their tertianship immediately after Christmas. Van Quickenborne and De Theux followed the program along with them. Van Quickenborne served as master of tertians. After the long retreat, they scattered for Lent. Van Quickenborne went out to work among the Osages.

A short time later, Bishop Rosati asked Van Quickenborne to staff the Saint Louis College which had opened in 1818. Van Quickenborne agreed. He began the initial Jesuit "drive" in St. Louis. During the first year, 1828-1829, the students boarded at Florissant. By the fall of 1829, the new college buildings at Ninth and Washington were ready. Twenty-nine-year-old Verhaegen became president of the college and local superior. But Van Quickenborne reserved to himself final decision in all matters. He made a weekly trip from Florissant to St. Louis to supervise activities. Two years later, the Jesuit General appointed Verhaegen superior of the St. Louis community and De Theux superior of the Missouri Mission, now independent of Maryland.

Van Quickenborne's troubles up to that point had been a combination of two things: first, the manpower shortage which brought him, a man of little administrative skill, into the position of acting superior; and second, his utter inability to delegate the least authority or to share responsibility with anyone else.

Now he was able to go out and do distinctive work on his own. He missionized many towns in the fast-growing Midwest. Wherever he went in Missouri and Illinois, he created a feeling of community among the Catholics who were usually a minority. He built the framework of the parish to come, a rallying point for all Catholics in a given area.

All the while his main objective had been to work among the Indians in the West. In 1832 he had penned a memorandum on this matter, which was communicated to Father General Roothaan in Rome. His chief points were

22

that the Indian missions had been the main purpose of the
Jesuit venture into Missouri; that the agreement with
Bishop DuBourg so obliged them; that it would be an
"image" factor in enlisting candidates and contributions;
that money had been received from Austria, Belgium, and
France for missions already presumed in operation; and,
lastly, that the Indians, the General of the Jesuits, and
the President of the United States all wanted the project.
More important practically, determined Van Quickenborne
wanted it. Finally in 1836, he was able to begin a
mission among the Kickapoo Indians in the vicinity of the
present-day Leavenworth in northeast Kansas.

This mission of Van Quickenborne was not destined to
endure or to accomplish great things. But it was the
first significant Indian mission begun by a Missouri
Jesuit. (Van Quickenborne's trips to the Osage had not
led as yet to anything permanent.) It became the fore-
runner of the many missions of Fr. De Smet among the
Indians of the Northwest, and presaged the whole great
story of Jesuit activity there.

In July of 1837 Van Quickenborne was recalled from
the Kickapoo Mission. In less than a month, on August
17, at the age of forty-nine, he died at Portage des
Sioux following an attack of fever that his wornout
constitution could not resist. In his death the Missouri
Mission lost its chief organizer and most valued worker.

Through fourteen long and difficult years Van Quickenborne spent himself on the Missouri Mission. His
patient endurance of hardships, his limitless zeal and
unwavering devotion to the cause of the Indians were the
marks of a great missionary. But along with these good
qualities went limitations of temperament which kept him
from working with others and carrying to completion many
of the works he had planned and begun so well. It was in
adversity and failure, however, that his real character
was revealed. His immediate and wholehearted acceptance
of the order to return from the Kickapoo Mission--the
great ambition of his life--was worthy of a true Jesuit.
His was the work of the pioneer, of the first wave of an
assault force. Others would build on the foundation he
had laid, on the beachhead he had secured at the junction
of the great rivers in midwestern America.

A PRIEST FOR ALL REASON

"Desegregation" from
St. Louis Post-Dispatch, August 29, 1980

I read with interest the August 24 special report on desegregation in the Post-Dispatch. On the last page, I found these words: "You've just finished a comprehensive report on St. Louis school desegretation..."

No, Mr. Editor, I had not read a "comprehensive report on St. Louis school desegregation." I found a report, possibly comprehensive, though many aspects did not receive adequate coverage, of public school education.

In another city where non-tax supported education, especially church-based education, is peripheral, editors might equate education with public education. This is not possible in St. Louis. Private education was part of the city's life before public educational institutions began. In fact, city, state and nation offered subsidies to these church-affiliated schools in the days of President Monroe.

The Post-Dispatch further, has often recognized the influence of the late Cardinal Ritter in integration in St. Louis. He opened parochial schools to blacks seven years before Brown vs. Topeka. The vast majority of Catholic people in the area accepted this decision.

The desegregation feature does not mention Cardinal Ritter. It carries one photograph of an unidentified group coming out of an unspecified building. The caption states: "In 1947, discussions began on whether to admit black students to Catholic schools in the St. Louis area." This is simply wrong. Shortly after his transfer here from Indianapolis, where he had integrated the schools, Cardinal Ritter insisted on the equality of all members of a parish. This meant an end to segregated schools. The church did not inaugurate "discussions" on the question. Protests arose from a number of people; and a few meetings were held under the impression that the laws of Missouri forbade integration. In all fairness to these people, the Post-Dispatch could have mentioned that in the end they accepted the decision; and, in fact, one of the leaders of the group became an outspoken advocate of integration in the intervening years.

"Woman in a Free Society"
from The Destiny of Modern Woman

Despite the pleasant sound of its name, nineteenth-century liberalism was a society-shaking movement which attempted to remove the individual from restraint or compulsion of any kind, not only from man-made law and tradition but also from the law of God. Its aspects were intellectual, economic, political, and religious. Intellectually, it championed free thought. Economically, it extolled the advance in production brought about by the industrial revolution and advocated complete freedom of individual enterprise, unhampered by any outside interference. Politically, it stood for constitutional government at home and favored the freeing of oppressed and enslaved peoples abroad.

Though inclined to look on religion as a harmless, personal affair, liberalism was hostile to all authoritative religion and especially to what it considered the apex of obscurantism and the chief enemy of freedom of thought, the papacy. The Vatican, in turn, offered no easy compromise. In the Syllabus of Errors issued in 1864, Pope Pius IX condemned the proposition that "the Roman Pontiff can and should reconcile himself with Progress, Liberalism, and modern Civilization." Six years later the Vatican Council, flying in the face of the liberals who rejected all authority, defined the doctrine of papal infallibility, that the Pope cannot err when speaking ex cathedra in matters of faith and morals.

Liberalism had its roots in the eighteenth-century philosophy and the French Revolution on the one side and the industrial revolution on the other. Drawing on the revolutionary ideas of total equality of all men and the unlimited freedom of the individual, liberalism developed a strongly individualistic philosophy. If every individual were free and equal, there could be no family, because the family organization demands authority and grades of respect. In large segments of society the industrial revolution had weakened the family as an economic unit, by taking the housewife from her home and in many instances pitting her against males as an economic rival. It thus gave cogency to the doctrinaire liberal's tenet that the individual was the unit of society. Further, for the woman of means it provided labor-saving devices that helped release her from work in the home and allowed her time for other activities.

Thus it was as a part of the liberal movement that feminism developed. This social philosophy sought for women a wider sphere of social opportunity as individuals rather than as members of a family unit, and it introduced a dual role into the lives of many women by adding to their duties as wives and mothers the possibility of activity beyond the home.

At the time of the French Revolution, individual women in England and France had complained against their status, which had been so restricted since the middle of the seventeenth century. But all efforts availed little and all protests made slight headway until the appearance of John Stuart Mill's Subjection of Women in 1869. This member of the English parliament, who because of his aunt-like manner was dubbed by Disraeli "the finishing governess," contributed little more than his name to this work. Though it reflected his ideas, it is generally known that his wife wrote most of it. But his name and support were enough. With the book's appearance not only had women found a champion, but those liberals who had been supporting the cause of "enslaved" peoples could not resist the challenge to emancipate women from "slavery." The feminist movement now began to progress in Europe and took on new life in America.

Though Mill's book is shot through with an egalitarian philosophy that tried to picture woman not as complementary to but as identical with man, the type of feminism that it helped to stimulate in English and American countries paid less attention to the ideological aspects of the woman question and concentrated its attention on a practical program of political and legal reforms. One would expect these regions to prove fertile fields for the demands of women, since in them parliamentary institutions existed and greater numbers of men were gradually winning the franchise. In these countries, too, the industrial revolution had brought about economic, social, and domestic changes that made emendations in woman's public status imperative. If large numbers of married women were wage earners, should they not be entitled by law to their own earnings? Should they not be able to make contracts and bring suits? Should they not be able to control and dispose of their separate property?

The invention of labor-saving devices made work in the home less time-consuming and gave many English and

American women leisure for other occupations. Many women of the upper middle and wealthy classes devoted their attention to activities of a cultural, religious, recreational, or political nature. They were to take part, too, in the Women's Club movement, which was to grow so rapidly in the latter part of the century.

Small beginnings of legal, political, educational, and economic changes, harbingers of greater victories to follow, came shortly after the appearance of Mill's book. The American territory of Wyoming gave its women the vote in 1869, and the first American woman lawyer was admitted to the bar in the same year. During the following year, the first European woman, a native of Holland, was allowed to follow her American sister's example, and the English parliament recognized the right of married women to hold property. At the same time, United States and Holland admitted women to the practice of medicine, as did England in 1876. The grade school systems, which were to provide equal educational opportunity for boys and girls, were now entering the adolescent stage. Two years before Mill's book, the University of Zurich had already led the way among European universities in admitting women. In that same year the University of Wisconsin gave great impetus to the rise of coeducation in America.

Early writers in the new science of sociology gave a supposedly solid anthropological basis for the new feminism by their studies in primitive society. Lewis H. Morgan, for instance, emphasized the importance of women in primitive tribal life, while discussing the evolution of civilization in his Ancient Society, published in 1877. After putting forth a theory of the natural superiority of the female sex, Lester F. Ward went on to appeal for the complete freedom of women, asserting that "the equality of the sexes will be the regeneration of humanity." With this, full-fledged feminism had its rationale.

Out of nineteenth-century liberalism grew another theory, socialism, the basic idea of which was state ownership of the means of production and exchange. How this development from liberalism to socialism took place is not of concern there. What matters is that socialism accepted many of the fundamental tenets of the liberal stand on feminism. Marx spurred the trend. Engels, Kautsky, Liebknecht, and above all, Bebel, whose writings will be discussed more at length later, followed his example. The socialists, also, had an added reason for championing woman's cause. Of this reason Carlton J.H. Hayes writes, "Let Socialists espouse the emancipation of women and women will be foes of capitalism and devotees of socialism." Evaluating this platform, he states," And the ensuing numerous enrollment of women in the several Marxian parties proved the soundness of this new tactic." The continent of Europe was the field of operation of these radical feminists, as it was of socialists and theorists in general.

Thus two wings of feminism grew up. Continental radicals concerned themselves with abstract theory and a feminist ideology; English and American radicals concentrated their attention on practical reforms of a political or legal nature. The former group was interested in liberty in the abstract; the latter, in liberties in the concrete, such as the vote, the removal of legal disabilities, and the like. The former demanded equality with man; the latter sought equal opportunities and privileges in education, occupations, the voting booth, parliament, and the courts of law.

"The Mississippi River Valley
and Westward Expansion"
from The Jesuit Bulletin, September, 1976

On May 17, 1673, Father Marquette set out with Louis Jolliet on the expedition to discover the source of the Mississippi River. On June 17 they reached an Arkansas Indian village, far enough to prove the great river did not flow westward but into the Gulf of Mexico. At this point the expedition turned back.

With Jolliet, Marquette laid the basis for France's claim to the Mississippi. To execute his plan for occupation of the whole Valley, Count Frontenac chose the explorer LaSalle, who reached the mouth of the Mississippi on April 7, 1682, claiming possession of the Valley in the name of the King. But in spite of an aggressive policy of commercial and military expansion, the first important settlements grew out of missionary efforts. By the time the French made their control of the Mississippi fairly secure, the great waterway had become a good artery of communication and trade.

On February 11, 1764, Pierre Laclede and party, following the broad waters of the Mississippi, took possession of the territory that is now the city of St. Louis and gave it that name. A fur trading post until the Louisiana Purchase of 1804, St. Louis' real development began with the arrival of the first steamboat in 1817. From this time on its river connections made the city the most important point in the Trans-Mississippi West. This close connection with many thousand miles of navigable highways decided the history of the city.

A familiar figure in the westward movement for more than three decades was Fr. Peter De Smet, S.J., one of the first members of the Missouri Province founded in 1823. Two things brought him into frequent relations with the Government, his intimate knowledge of the Far West and his influence with the Indians. As an explorer, geographer, author, and peace negotiator he scored remarkable success, but first and foremost he was a friend of the redman. It was missionary zeal on behalf of the Indians that drew him to the West and made the West dear to him until his dying day.

Before the decision was made to locate the Gateway Arch at St. Louis as part of the Jefferson National Expansion Memorial, there appeared in The Historical Bulletin of St. Louis University in 1934 an editorial by Fr. Raymond Corrigan, S.J., giving historical reasons why St. Louis should be the site:

"There is a project afoot for a National Expansion Memorial. There are strong reasons for placing such a monument on the Mississippi at St. Louis. Now is the time to perpetuate the pioneer spirit, to set before the eyes of all the world a monument which in dignity and artistic perfection will embody our consciousness of our greatness as a nation...

"St. Louis was once admittedly the 'Gateway to the West.' Through it passed the surging humanity that traveled the Oregon Trail, the Overland Trail, the Santa Fe Trail. All roads led to St. Louis from the East or from St. Louis to the West... The visitor from foreign lands should find on the banks of the world-renowned river a memorial to the explorer, the trapper, the Indian fighter, the fur trader, the pioneer farmer, the missionary, the business man, the railroad builder of the Frontier as well as the statesman and financial backer, to the unknown thousands and the few outstanding individuals who carried through the magnificent epic of national expansion."

"Lincoln's Thanksgiving Proclamation"
a sermon previously unpublished

Thanksgiving Day was a local celebration until 1863 when in early October President Lincoln issued a great state paper that foreshadlowed the Gettysburg address of the following month and the second inaugural seventeen months later.

The time was not overwhelmingly happy. The Union forces had beaten Lee at Gettysburg but Lee had escaped to familiar ground with his army intact. Vicksburg had fallen in early July but the Union Army of the Cumberland had just suffered a staggering defeat at Chickamauga in Georgia and had retreated. The War remained uncertain, the survival of the Union a question.

Yet Lincoln could count the nation's blessings. Foreign Powers had refrained from hitting us while we were down; commerce throve; fields flourished; the population grew; the nation expanded; only the embattled areas--a relatively small section of our giant nation-- did not enjoy prosperity. The Heavenly Father had indeed shown Himself bountiful. In a challenge to all that pre-saged the ideals of his second inaugural, Lincoln asked the people to return thanks in prayer and to express penitence for our national perverseness; to commend to God's tender care all those who had become widows, orphans, mourners or sufferers in the lamentable civil strife--and to ask God to heal the nation's wounds and return it to a situation more conducive to His Divine purposes for mankind--peace, harmony, tranquillity, and union.

We can add little to President Lincoln's goals and ideals; Thanksgiving is not so much a day or a season; but an attitude and an acknowledgement; an attitude of gratefulness, and an acknowledgement that all these good things came from God.

"The Spirit that Built the West"
from Frontier, January 15, 1950

The rugged individualist built the American West.

30

The self-reliant man of the frontier, who pushed off into the wilderness and without help from a distant government in Washington, carved out a new empire. Such is the picture that by steady repetition is gaining constantly wider acceptance.

Having built up this theory as the pattern of the past that made America great, its supporters use the "don't-change-the-winning-combination" argument. Just as an athletic coach leaves a victorious team in the game, even though he feels a different combination might be doing even better, so, they argue, we should not change this "traditionally American way" that has brought us a higher standard of living than any other nation in the world.

Yet this picture is not true. A careful historical analysis gives a different verdict. Resourceful individuals, it must be admitted, played a not inconsiderable part in the development of the West. But cooperation rather than competitive individualism was the prevailing spirit of the frontier. Then too, a big-brotherly governmnet, that never overstepped its function by making the West its ward, was always on hand with help.

Americans today are determining policies of untold consequence for the future West--policies on the development of our great river valleys, on the use of water for irrigation, on the spread of electrical power, on the holding of land. The social philosophy of the planners will have great influence in shaping this vast segment of our nation. It is imperative that they view the history of Western development as it really took place.

Certain general patterns appear from a merely cursory glance at Western American history. Who were the real rugged individuals of the early West? There was John Colter, a lone-wolf by nature, who liked to wander off from the expedition with which he started out and became the first white man to view the geysers of the Yellowstone. There was Father De Smet, the Jesuit missionary, who frequently went out alone among the Flatheads and Coeur d'Alenes. There were famed marshals like Wyatt Earp of Tombstone and "Wild Bill" Hickok of Abilene, who did much to establish law and order in the rough country. But John Colter was not a builder of the West; Father De Smet travelled by himself because he had found that other white men brought along a "firewater" that had more effect on the Indians than the "hell-fire"

of his sermons; and the cooperative effort of the Vigi-
lantes more than matched the records of the famed marshals.

Pioneer Cooperation

Just try to picture Mr. Rugged Individualist driving
his lone covered wagon through the lands of the Sioux and
the Cheyenne, or building the entire Union Pacific Railroad by himself, or bringing Oregon from Wildneress to
statehood.

Rather the vision of the long covered wagon train
with many families traveling together for protection ring
truer. Did not the close grouping of homes around a fort
or stockade precede thier dispersal over the countryside?
Was it not a familiar western tradition for all neighbors
to participate in the "house-raising" of a newcomer? The
story of the Mormons is one of cooperation in building
Zion in the wilderness.

The tycoons behind the railroad to the Pacific could
not have pushed the track ten miles without the Irish
roadbuilders coming from the East and the Chinese from
the West. Granted the influence of many outstanding
individuals, and the individual courage of tens of thousands, especially the pioneer mothers, the only histori-
cally sound conclusion is that cooperation built the
West. Recent historians recognize an individualism on
the frontier, but it was cooperative rather than competitive. They see 'a combination of resourceful individual
effort with an ability to work freely with one's neighbor.

Only in the range cattle industry of the Eighties,
did a ruthless rugged individualism appear. The normal
market for food and leather drove the prices of cattle
upward and the speculation mania spread faster than the
hoof-and-mouth disease. Absentee owners squeezed out the
small local cattleman and expanded the business far beyond the margin of safety. But the cattlemen fought not
only their competitors in business. They likewise engaged in a struggle with the farmers pushing west with the
railroad lines. Yes, the early cattlemen were frequently
rugged, ruthless and individualistic; but they do not
destroy the general pattern.

When late in the nineteenth century, rugged individualism ran the American government according to its own whims, the farmers of the West, in alliance with the agrarian South, rose up in a desperate attempt to drive the men of industry and money from the capital of our country. These Populists sought a reorientation of government in the interests of agriculture that would have implied the end of laissez-faire capitalism (or rugged individualism, or "free enterprise"), government ownership of railroads, careful control of natural resources by the central government, and for the operation of the financial system for the greater benefit of the farming class. Had the Populists won a thorough victory, they would have wiped out the gains of the rugged individualists since the Civil War. And Populism was a grass-roots movement of western people!

The Spanish Influence

What part did the government plan in building the West? Three of its greatest states, Texas, New Mexico, and California, were orginally opened up for settlement as part of the expansion program of the Spanish Empire. Self-reliant though he was, the likeable Franciscan, Fray Junipero Serra, who strung his missions like rosary-beads along the coast from San Diego to Monterey, could not be claimed by the rugged individualists.

When Jefferson purchased the Louisiana Territory (almost half of the West) in 1803, the tradition of government interest did not cease, though it was not marked by the excessive paternalism of Spanish rule. Jefferson's first act was to send an expedition under Meriwether Lewis and William Clark to explore the new addition to the United States.

The first great industry beyond the Mississippi was the fur trade. Here the rugged individualists--in this case John Jacob Astor-worked hard to "get the government out of business." Why? For the better running of the fur industry? Hardly. Any historian knows that the government's purpose in establishing the so-called "factories," to which the Indians could bring their pelts, was to give the redskin a fair deal. Astor wanted to exploit the Indian with rum and whiskey,--and did! The plans of other rugged individualists, likewise, were not always designed to build, but more frequently to exploit the western lands. Witness the early years of the American foresting industry.

The presence of the United States army was another example of the government's solicitude for its western territories. There was a limit to which the free effort of the frontiersman and even the territorial militia could go in fighting hostile Indians.

The rugged individualist welcomed the government's help in pushing railroads to the Pacific. Both the Central Pacific, working inland from California, and the Union Pacific, coming from the Missouri River, had indispensable aid from Washington. They were given a right of way, grants of twenty square miles of public land for each mile of rail, and loans of $16,000 a mile for construction on the level country, two times that much in the foothills, and three times that sum in the mountain ranges.

The Great Land Grants

The Santa Fe received a land grant of 6400 acres for every mile built. The Northern Pacific, planned to connect Lake Superior with Puget Sound, likewise enjoyed governmental patronage both in the State of Minnesota and in the territories from there to the Pacific. In all, the railroads received an amount of land almost equal in size to pre-Hitler Germany.

Nor did all the government's help in land go the the corporations building railroads. The Homestead Act of May, 1862, gave to the heads of families or other adult individuals 160 acres of land. Final title could be gained after a five-year residence and some indication of improvement.

It would not be true to suggest that no other motive than interest in the homesteader prompted the government to pass this bill. The Republicans in control of both houses of Congress wanted to be witnesses of a political wedding of the East and West. The growing industry of the seaboard states sought another market for its manufacturers. Still the motives were not exclusively economic. There were men like Congressman George W. Julian of Indiana, one of the chief supporters of the Homestead Bill, who pushed it for idealistic reasons.

Since the beginning of the new century, the federal

government has taken an active interest in the irrigation of arid areas of the West. With the vigorous support of President Theodore Roosevelt, the Reclamation Law of 1902 was enacted by Congress. This law not only gave government help to the arid areas, but set up a farsighted policy in the use of water for irrigation. A study of the intention of those drawing up the Act shows these four pillars of that policy: 1) acreage limitation in order that the water might benefit as many owner-operators as possible; 2) both partial and complete irrigation, as the farms required; 3) irrigation of private as well as public lands; 4) the breaking up of large private holdings, especially those owned by absentees or used for speculative purposes. Such was the history of western development...

This true pattern must be made the foundation of our planning for the future West, not only out of respect for successful tradition, but because it properly recognizes the function of the individual, the community and the national government. Resourceful individuals can do much, both by themselves and with others, the Coronados, the Hills of a modern day. But cooperation must always and will always have its place. And lastly, recognizing its proper sphere, which is to promote the general welfare not by absorbing but by encouraging and supplementing local effort, the government can make those laws most necessary for the full development of the future West.

Father Faherty is Professor of History at Saint Louis University, Director of the St. Stanislaus Museum, and English Language Co-ordinator of the Encyclopedia of Jesuit History.

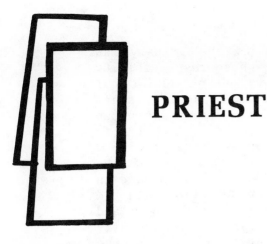

PRIEST

When Christ sent his disciples to spread His word, telling them to leave behind their earthly comforts and attachments, He gave some tough orders. Father Barnaby Faherty's vision of the priesthood springs clearly from a response to that command and a hard earned understanding of its demands. He uses his writing as a means to examine for himself and others what the priesthood is -- not from the philosopher's perspective, but from the working priest's perspective. He is interested both in the social role of the priest and in the very personal question of what it feels like to serve as a priest. The following selections from Faherty's writing provide a picture of the priest's life; in them he writes both as a priest (as in Living Alone) and about priests -- real and fictional.

Young priests, as young professionals in many fields, believe that they can change the world. Father Faherty knows this. In the short story "Letter of Protest," he represents both a brash idealist priest mocking his bishop and a socially conscious pastor defending principle. And he shows his own early idealism in the excerpt from a letter to Leo Weber, S.J., as he looks back from a perspective of thirty years on his own personal attempts to change the world.

The sermon "Micah" and the article "One-Man Point Four" contain another important element in Father Faherty's view of the priest's role. For

A PRIEST FOR ALL REASON

Barnaby Faherty, the priest is an ordinary man with an extraordinary calling whose responsibility it is to do his best anyway. Heroes exist, of course, but they work on a small scale: small frogs in small ponds who achieve important human results.

This same belief that a priest is an ordinary man allows for the very human picture of the priesthood in the story "His Crucial Hour" and in the excerpt from A Wall for San Sebastian. In the first, Father Faherty chuckles at the fears and nervousness of a young priest (perhaps not so different from himself as a young man), and, in the scene between Fray Leon and Kinita, he portrays the very human struggles of a priest who feels an unpriestly affection for one of his flock.

All of these elements, however, find balance in a sense of stability in his role as a priest. The man who has forsaken his home and family to do God's work develops a new and certain sense of home, both in place and in spirit. Father Faherty's description of the home chapel of his student years shows one aspect of this new home. Fray Leon's thoughts on the mission of San Sebastian present another, a priest's growing sense that his home is his work. The resulting calm arises from a careful, critical and willing acceptance of the church's basic vision, its underlying values and beliefs. In Chapter Five of Living Alone, Father Faherty calls upon this foundation, this certainty in his role as teacher, counselor, spiritual advisor. The brash idealism of the priest Frank Mull from "Letter of Protest" is exchanged for genuine human sympathy. The preachiness and righteousness of the young priest character, out to defend the underdog on his own disappear, replaced by the security of a working priest who understands that most people (priests included) are underdogs and that the whole Church's goal and the priest's duty is to help them.

from "Letter of Protest"
previously unpublished

The Bishop began his interminable message on the "Personnel Problem." In other dioceses they called it "The Vocation Crisis." Frank Mull had almost memorized it. The

38

Bishop has been giving it ever since he was consecrated. It
annoyed Frank. Never once did the Bishop ever say that a
young person might be of service to others, or gain a high
place in heaven by committing his life to Christ. It was
always the latest figure on the needs of the diocese. But
then, Frank thought, it didn't really matter, since most of
his people understood no English anyway. They just listened
in the hope that if they didn't learn their religion, at
least they might learn a word or two of English.

Finally, the Bishop ended the sermon. A short time
later, he had confirmed the children and the two adults.
The priests returned to the sacristy. The Bishop waited
until Dean Trittleiter had left the room before he accosted
the pastor.

"Father Mull," Bishop Dahl said, "do you have permission for the Mass in Spanish?"

"Your Excellency, I have permission for the Mass in the
language of the people. My people speak Spanish."

"We are living in the United States of America, Father.
If these people don't know English, they should learn it."

"I think that's a splendid idea, Your Excellency. I'll
tell them to learn English so the next time you come and
give a sermon, they can understand what you're talking
about."

The Bishop walked out the sacristy door.

"Take it easy, Frank," Carlow said. "You were pretty
rough. Little 'Kewpie' can't take that sort of thing."
[ed. note: Carlow refers to his bishop as "Kewpie Dahl"
several times in the story.]

"Paulinus will be leaving us soon," Frank said. "We
are getting a new auxiliary. Paulinus will have a chance to
bestow the blessing of his presence on some other fortunate
group of American people."

"I'd be inclined to laugh," Carlow said, "if it wasn't
so damned tragic." He walked toward the rectory.

Frank Mull turned out the lights in the Church, greeted
the few stragglers who still remained in front, and walked
to the rectory. Turner and Carlow argued about Vatican II
in one corner of the front room. The Bishop talked to the
Monsignor.

"Excuse me, Monsignor," Bishop Dahl said. "I must have
a word with Father Mull before I leave."

"Do you wish to go to my office, Your Excellency?"
Mull asked.

The Bishop looked up at big Frank Mull and decided to
enjoy the security of a large group. "It will be fine here,
Father." He paused, assumed his most pontifical air, and
went on. "Do you know Charles Carroll?"

"No, I believe he died," Frank said with feigned reflection. "I think he signed the Declaration of Independence and outlived all other signers. But he finally died before I got to meet him."

"That wasn't really funny, Father. I refer to Father Charles Carroll, late of the Augustine University faculty."

"Oh! That Charles Carroll! No, I don't know him."

"Have you ever read any of his books?"

"Oh, no, Your Excellency. No, I haven't read any of his books. Have you?"

"Then how in God's name have you come to be endowed with the background to write a public criticism of the Bishop's committee on the University because it no longer requires the services of this unqualified person."

"Paulinus, my friend, have you ever heard of Ignacio Revelacion and Juan Bautista Carmel?"

"No! Father! But they certainly have Catholic names!"

"They do that indeed, Paulinus. I'll tell you who they are. They are parishoners of mine who shovel manure all day in Alamo Park. They put the manure around the cottonwood trees so they grow faster." Frank Mull always stood six feet two tall but now he towered over the little Bishop. He smiled broadly and went one. "Now Ignacio Revelacion and Juan Bautista Carmel cannot be fired without a hearing. What's good enough for those fine manure-shovelers in my parish is certainly good enough for a priest of God."

Non-plussed, the Biship could only retreat. "Good evening, gentlemen," he said. "We will discuss this matter more at length later." His secretary picked up his suitcase and followed the Bishop to his Cadillac.

Micah
an invocation

Twenty seven hundred years ago, a young man of a desert tribe of the Near East felt a call to speak out in the name of the one true God, to proclaim, to prophecy, as a few men of his tribe were wont to do. He had one difficulty, however in getting a hearing, one out of the ordinary run of difficulties. Another prophet lived, the most poetic, the most positive of all the prophets, the one who added the dimension of foretelling to the proclamation and witness of the earlier great prophets. That man's name was Isaiah. He told of the Messiah to come, the wonderful counsellor, almighty God, prince of peace, Father of the World to come. We still thrill to the words of Isaiah 2700 years later.

To prophecy in Isaiah's time was like trying to gain

recognition as an orator when the voice of Daniel Webster still resounded through the United States Senate or, in my profession, to be on the same platform with Dr. Billy Graham or Pope John Paul II.

Yet that other prophet spoke out at the same time as Isaiah. Even though we had Daniel Webster, we could still heed his fellow statesman, Henry Clay. Even in the hey-dey of Bishop Sheen, we could still learn from our own pastor. Even though we listen to Isaiah, we can profit from that other spokesman for God. That prophet's name was Micah. No Isaiah he! But he had his moment. He offered a question often asked by sages of old. And he gave an answer that rings down unchallenged through 27 centuries.

The question: with what gift shall I come into God's presence? His answer:

This is what God asks of you:
Only this, to act justly,
to love tenderly
and to walk humbly with your God.

Heavenly Father, we ask you, as we begin these deliberations, that we can today, and every day, follow the advice of the Prophet Micah, and to act justly, love tenderly and walk humbly with our God.

from a letter to the
Very Reverend Leo F. Weber, S.J.
previously unpublished

Almost 20 years ago, after consultation with the Chicano leaders in the Colorado area, I recommended that the social science division of Regis College build a program that would make Regis the place where the Chicanos would look to for guidance in solving the issues facing them. At the time I had served for several years as Chaplain of the Colorado Conference of Latin American Groups. I was in touch with all the leaders -- Catholic and non-Catholic -- among the Hispanic people. They all insisted that only a Catholic School could gain the response and following needed for such a program. They went over with me the reasons why Regis could do the job more effectively than other schools, such as St. Michael's, now the College of Santa Fe, or Loyola in Los Angeles or St. Mary's in San Antonio.

As a trial run of what we had in mind, we ran a seminar during the course of a semester. We brought in as speakers the leading men -- Anglo and Hispanic -- in the affairs of

the Chicano community. I offered to seek the funds needed
to support the program and submitted the entire proposal
through one of the consultors of the house who was personally interested. Even the Provincial at the time, Father
Joseph Fisher, expressed interest in the proposal but the
authorities at Regis never so much as acknowledged the sub-
mission of this plan. Think what this would have meant for
Regis, the Chicanos, the good of the Church and the glory of
God.

"One-Man Point Four"
from The Credit Union Bridge, May, 1954

Such was the land of British Honduras...(when Father
Ganey arrived)
The people were not overburdened with the goods of this
world; the wage scales scraped the bottom of the Caribbean.
"Loan sharks" -- of an especially vicious tropical variety -- took advantage of the people's needs, growing rich on
interest rates which reached twenty-five cents on the dollar
or higher.
True, Belize had a bank. Like most banks, however, it
was not geared to receive small savings from poor people and
to extend loan facilities to them. Much less could it provide small character loans without security.
Several American priests working in British Honduras
began to ask themselves: "How can people really live the
full Christian life when the loan shark has joined the wolf
at the threshold?"
How can these poor people think of God, or progress in
Christian life if their constant thoughts center on money
worries? While we talk, this thought engrosses their minds:
MY RENT IS DUE TOMORROW...
One of the missionaries who asked such questions was
the perennially youthful-looking veteran, Father Marion
Ganey of Punta Gorda, in the southern part of the Province.
He knew it was easy to tell his people what to do, but that
results of this method did not last. It was hard to keep
asking: "What are you going to do about your problems?"
But this question Father Ganey continued to ask until they
had determined to do something. Only then did he suggest
that they form a credit union.
Would they be interested, Father Ganey wondered. Would
they understand what he was trying to propose? After all,
their experience in handling money was limited, and the
credit union program seemed at first a jungle of intricate
procedures. He had no examples in the colony to point to.

His people could not say: "Our neighbors in the next village have done this. Why can't we?" His task was like hacking a new road through a section of the bush hitherto isolated.

Yet the people of Punta Gorda stuck with their missionary teacher. Careful study led them to the conclusion: This is what we will do. And so in 1943 the first credit union in British Honduras took its initial toddling steps. They named it for St. Peter Claver, the man who first taught Christianity to many of the Caribbean Negroes.

The St. Peter Claver Credit Union hacked a new road to economic stability through the Belize bush. Not long afterwards, others were trying the new path...

A fellow missionary of Father Ganey, Father H. Sutti, the first graduate of Boys Town, Nebraska, to follow the sacred ministry, began a study group at Corozal, at the opposite tip of the colony. The credit union program was not something new to him, since long before he had started a study club among the children of Belize. His group began a credit union on the "learn-while-we-go" plan.

Before the end of the year about twenty members had collected their pennies, until the coins "mountained" to thirty dollars. Every Thursday the members gathered to learn more about the workings of their credit union, which they placed under the patronage of St. Francis Xavier, apostle of the Indies.

When Father Sutti was transferred to the south of the colony, Corozal was lucky in having Fernando Villamor arrive from Jamaica. While there, he had studied the vigorous credit union movement, launched some time before, and continually inspirited by that human dieselengine, Father John Peter Sullivan, a popular speaker at credit union league conventions in North America.

Under Villanor's guidance, the Corozal Credit Union mounted to two hundred members, its assets reached seven thousand dollars, and it had loaned almost twenty-one thousand dollars by the middle of 1950...

In the meantime the superior of the Mission (and now Bishop of Belize), the Very Reverend David Hickey, S.J., had attended the Mission Institute sponsored by the Institute of Social Order at St. Louis University, and gave the encouragement of his presence to many discussions of credit unions. Sunbright days lay ahead for the movement.

Not long afterward Father Ganey was freed from other duties to devote his full time to the advancement of the credit union movement in British Honduras. With the valuable on-the-spot assistance of other mid-western born priests, Father William Moore and Father William V. Ulrich, organizations sprang up from Yucatan to the southern tip of the colony.

One of these groups deserves special comment, the Holy Redeemer Credit Union of the capital city, which was destined to become the largest by far in the entire colony. By the end of 1950 it included four hundred members, and had loaned out seventy-two thousand dollars.

These undramatic statistics may seem, in comparison with some of the credit unions here at home, like tropical seedlings in the midst of full-grown oak trees; yet they mean far more in view of the comparative economic situation of the people they serve.

Behind them, as behind all Belize credit union figures, hides a story of departed worries, of improved homes, of stabilized family finances, of health restored through medical care which had hitherto been impossible, of life made brighter in countless little ways, and of a more vital service of God. Loan sharks were seeking more favorable hunting waters...

"His Crucial Hour"
from The Southwest Courier, Spring 1944

Father Rell walked gingerly up the steps of the forbidding St. Patrilla's Convent. He felt like a bush-leaguer facing Mort Cooper for the first time. But then again -- reassuring, wasn't it? -- the Cantian Sisters of the Strict Observence did not realize what faced them either. This was the young priest's first retreat.

For years he had anticipated his initial retreat. Yes, ever since his senior high year when he decided to climb the sheer course of the priesthood. But this type of retreat had never entered his mind!

Older fathers had cushioned him for the ordeal. But it had seemed too unreal then. Now he was face to face with the unavoidable struggle.

Would anyone be at the door to meet him? No! Just as the veternas had warned, a paper pinned to an inner door directed him to the room he was to occupy. Down the corridor he went, past the bishop's room. His Excellency was not there at the time, but a room in the uncloistered part of the house was always reserved for him. On he inched, seeking room Number 6. No sound of life disturbed the dim corridor. Just like the long walk at the state "pen" the morning of an execution, he thought.

"Ah, there it is! Number 6, second from the end, north side. The dim light of a small high window caused him un-

44

thinkingly to recite a few lines of the Prisoner of Chillon. A chair, a prie-dieu, a bed -- with mattress, thank God! -- emphasized the bareness of the apartment. He felt like the Big Dipper with its handle below the horizon.

"Umph -- just like the Southwalk Country Club," he said to reassure himself. "Except no golf course. But that can be remedied." He glanced rapidly at the schedule of spiritual exercises which lay on the chair. "Opening Discourse, 8 o'clock, Thursday. That's tonight," the priest said.

At the bottom, a map of the house showed him the way to the chapel. He would find his three meals in his room, at the close of Mass, examination of conscience, and Rosary.

"Cordial and cozy," he said aloud. "At least they eat in this cloistered community."

He went over his initial instruction before the window at the end of the hall, then said some Office. The zero hour rapidly closed in on him, like the Allies on Hitler. Following the directions of the local cartographer he eased down the corridor at three minutes to eight. There was the appointed door at his left.

"That doesn't look like a chapel," he said to himself. "But then again, how do I know that the Sisters of St. Patrilla's Convent want chapel doors to look like chapel doors?"

Cautiously, he turned the knob and pushed the door open. A long row of beds greeted his gaze. "I'm sorry," he said -- to the upholstery, for no one was present. His exit was rapid.

The third door he tried revealed the glow of the sanctuary lamp, warm and comforting, like the Southwind blowing across a snowy plain.

After fumbling a long time for the switch on the sacristy wall, he found it, as he had found the chapel door, exactly where directions had said it was. A small lamp lighted a desk in the sacristy. He looked at his watch. Two after eight.

The Sisters would be waiting, kneeling in quiet prayer, behind the huge grate that hid them from the priest's view. His shirt soaked up perspiration under his cassock. The beginning of his "Our Father" was half apologetic. Fortunately he remembered in time to say the entire prayer himself. He had been told that the Sisters did not answer the prayers vocally. He almost said Lord have mercy on me, in place of the ejaculation, Most Sacred Heart of Jesus.

Though no sound came from beyond the grill, the noise of the retreat master's chair scraping the floor reverberated through the chapel. He remembered the old teaching rule given in a college Education course: "Start right in as if you have been teaching all your life."

Long preparation carried the young guide of souls through a fine beginning. His first thoughts were on the Virgin, God's greatest creature. Yes, God's greatest creature was a woman. She led her life in quiet obscurity as most of the Sisters before him. He almost heard a sigh of satisfaction at his flattering tributes to womankind.

About half-way through he made his one blunder -- a joke. It was time for a bit of relaxation, he thought. Forty-five minutes is such a long time anyway. So he told a funny story. No one laughed! Yet Father let slip an uncontrollable half-laugh himself, which he tried to turn into a cough. A radiator knocked loudly, as if some invisible gunner were attempting to give the speaker just recompense for the lame story he told.

Time seeped by. Who ever said these talks had to be forty-five minutes in length? Repetition succeeded recapitulation. He invoked the saints to bless them. He told how pleased God was with their service. He called on more saints. Other cliches followed. The second hand trudged on, trying to ape the sluggish hour hand.

"Forty-five minutes or no forty-five minutes, I'm through!" he suddenly determined, and closed the talk.

It was over! It was over in capitals, underlined and with an exclamation point. The worst forty-five minutes he ever spent and ever hoped to spend. He hurried to his room and dropped on the bed. Only then did he realize the exhaustion his tenseness had brought on. He was through -- but the talk was over...

Fifteen minutes later there was a sharp knock at the door. He rose, brushed his cassock, and said, "Come in!"

The door opened. A nun stood at the threshold. "It's past time for the instruction, Father. The Sisters are waiting. Mother Superior sent me for you."

"But I gave it already! I - ah -- er -- the sign said eight o'clock."

"Oh, yes, Father," the unperturbed Sister responded, "we forgot to notify you that the Convent of St. Patrilla does not run on Daylight Time."

from A Wall for San Sebastian

A small hand reached up and clasped his, as little boys are wont to do. At first he thought nothing of it. Then suddenly he realized that someone else held the other hand of the little boy.

He turned. It was Kinita. She grasped her little brother's right hand, as the Padre held his left. Suddenly he realized that she was no longer a little girl. This was a mature young woman beside him.

He panicked for a moment as he reached the top of the ridge. He thought that everyone was looking at the three of them, and he wondered what people would be thinking. He casually looked at the crowd beside the lake. All were concerned with their own affairs. He regained his composure without betraying his inner disturbance. He stood erect and squared his shoulders.

The thought suddenly came to him that no one in the entire world meant more to him than she. The thought startled him. Yet on reflection, he knew it was true.

She had always had a taken-for-granted place in his affections. Something of a father's love for a child was in it; something of a spiritual guide's concern for a disciple; and something too -- he had to admit -- of personal affection. Yes, she meant more to him than anyone in the world.

Padre Leon was no woman-hater. Of the many women he had met as a priest and before as a soldier -- some were more beautiful than Kinita. Some smarter. One or two, perhaps, more immediately charming. But for a combination of qualities, she surpassed all.

Their meeting in this way had been a sheer accident. And yet he had to fight the thought that walking through life with her might have been a thrilling experience, had his vocation not been to the priesthood. Had I met her, he thought, before I decided to enter the novitiate -- but then he realized that had he not been a missionary he would never have known her at all.

Here I am a man of forty-five and she a girl of eighteen. I'm older than her father.

Kinita broke into his swift reflections. "I would like to ask you a question, mi padre," she began. Her voice drew him back from his headlong thoughts.

"Yes, my daughter," he said, and a slight flush came to his face. He tried to withdraw his hand causally from the little brother's strong grip. But the little boy held tight. What could she be asking? Padre Leon wondered.

"In a sermon last year you spoke of Saint Teresa," Kinita began, "You told how she loved and served God. I have thought much about her."

Kinita paused thoughtfully. Then she blurted out, "Could anyone be like her?"

Padre Leon slowly thought out the phrasing of his answer. "Yes, my daughter. If she loved God more than herself." They stood still on the top of the little knoll.

Kinita turned her gaze directly at the priest. "Could

I be like her? For a long time I have been thinking of it, mi padre. Do you think I could be a Sister?"

His words came with swiftness and finality. "I think you would make a wonderful nun!"

He turned and looked at the distant ridges to the southwest. In what strange ways God works. While I struggle to keep myself on the high road, God uses my words to help her aspire to the highest.

Thoughtfully and calmly he asked, "You of course understand the sacrifices entailed?"

"Yes, mi padre," her voice was calm, sure.

"You will have to give up home, parents, friends. You will have a life of hard work. Above all, you will never have a home, a husband, a family of your own. You will have to give up all human loves for the love of Christ."

"I know that, mi padre," she answered without hesitation. "I am willing to give up marriage." Her tone was objective, unemotional, business-like.

Padre Leon paused, groping in his mind for other important things to ask. "Have you talked to your parents?"

"I have mentioned it to them. They seem to be upset. But they will finally say 'yes.' Do not worry about that."

"Were you thinking of the Sisters in Durango or in Mexico City?"

"In Durango, mi padre."

"Keep praying and receiving the sacraments," he advised. "And in the meantime I will get in touch with the Bishop and the Sisters in Durango."

Kinita picked up her little brother and danced away. As she left, tears of wonder and happy regret filled the priest's eyes.

from "The Immaculata Chapel
and the Big Fire"
from The Jesuit Bulletin, October 1980

The Immaculata Chapel in St. Marys, Kansas, with its ivy covered belfry, its grey stone walls and sharply pointed red tile roof, overawes few people. It could fit without crowding into the Cathedrals of Saint Louis or Saint Paul.

Its beauty pales before San Xavier del Bac in the Arizona desert or the Priory Church in suburban Saint Louis.

It fails to blend with the encroaching Kansas wheat fields, as Santa Fe's Santuario El Cristo Rey seems to spring out of the brown earth of New Mexico.

This chapel casts its distinct spell. It is more than a matter of memory, as the setting of that great ceremony of ordination when the Bishop of Eastern Kansas placed his hands on the heads of sixty of us, as the Apostles long ago placed their hands on Paul and Barnabas and sent them forth to preach the Word.

Long before that day I felt the same as I do now. Whenever I return and see the Immaculata Chapel crowning the northern ridge of the Kaw Valley, I feel as a child who knows his mother is near, as a clipper under the shadow of its own dock, as a wanderer who had come home.

from A Wall for San Sebastian

Then Mexico City! The fabulous home of the Aztecs! Who was there without love for it?

Each place he had ever been had fascinated him for a time. Then he was ready to move on. That's why he had so enjoyed the trip to New Mexico. Now he was going back to San Sebastian. Yet he knew that after he had been there for a time, he would be ready to move on again. Maybe he was meant to move and wander and go from here to there, bringing a little light and encouragement; but he was glad there would always be a home port, and that home port had to be strengthened and fortified.

Then he began to think of Xavier, who traveled throughout the East, remaining nowhere for any length of time. Even on his deathbed on San Cian Island, the Saint was looking forward to the day he could enter the mainland of China. And Padre Eusebio Kino! The journeys he made throughout Sonora and Pimeria Alta! And Junipero Serra! The missions he had strung along the California coast!

It had been to serve in California that he, Leon Alastray, had first joined the Spanish Army. It had been to work in the California Mission that he chose the Franciscan Order.

Then Padre Leon realized it was not the place that mattered. San Sebastian was not simply a spot on the earth or even a Church. It was a group of people, who had tied themselves just a little bit more strongly to his heart than other people had; Kinita, first of all; Kinita who had helped him plant the first six pine trees -- four of which still grew in the corners of the courtyard; Kinita, who taught catechism so well; Kinita, whom he still thought of as a lithe girl of twelve, but who had, without his being aware of it, grown into young womanhood; and, her father Kino, trim, tough, challenging, a man with an edge; and Antonito who kept the Church as neat as himself was unkempt; who always agreed apologetically yet went ahead and did

things as he had previously decided; and Agueda and Dona
Donosa -- both nurturing sorrows but expressing that sorrow
in diverse ways; and the others.

That's why San Sebastian was home. That's why the
Visitante could say his heart was there.

"Portrait of a Happy Woman"
from Living Alone

She has a warm personal love for her Savior Jesus
Christ. She keeps the commandments. She is loyal to her
Church and its demands. Because she belongs to a "way of
life" group which inculcates a definite program of religious
living, she is more than ordinarily concerned about the
practices of devotion to God.

Naturally she had always wanted marriage. She survived
the usual number of teen-age infatuations. In her early
twenties she was deeply in love with a young man. They
wisely came to the mutual realization that they were not
really suited to each other.

Gradually she became reconciled to the single state.
One day, during a spiritual retreat, a whole new world opened to her. She learned to see the hand of her Heavenly
Father in all these events of her life. She realized clearly that this was the life God intended for her. With that
conviction a new and enlarged peace flooded her soul. She
has always known that happiness was not automatic or acci-
dental but that each individual had to achieve happiness.
She is building hers.

In her early twenties, recreation became almost a mania
with her. In summer she spent most of her free hours on the
golf course, in winter at the bowling alley. She wanted to
excel in both sports. Finally she came to two frank admis-
sions: first, that she did not quite have the needed native
ability; and secondly, that, even if she had such skill,
athletic prowess did not necessarily insure a pleasant time.
She came to enjoy widespread companionship on the golf
course and the bowling alley. Golf and bowling became
recreations, not weekend tasks.

Next, she acknowledged that games were not the only
means of recreation. She slowly developed a balance between
reading and sports, between cultural activities and community projects.

Her work has variety, novelty, freshness. It gives her
contact with many people, and especially with children in
their high school years. As book-consultant for all high
schools in the city, she travels from her office downtown to

give books talks at the schools. She promotes reading programs. She acquaints the students with books available in the respective branch libraries. She assists school librarians, if they should wish, in drawing up book lists and in coordinating the use of the school library with the public facilities. She has time to advise students personally on questions of literature or whatever else they might wish to ask. She sees the good results of her efforts.

Like all human beings, the people with whom she works are as varied as the jackets on the latest best sellers. Most are pleasant, some are difficult, a few downright disagreeable. She takes them all in stride.

The pay is good. She has security. She always looks to the most enjoyable side of her work. She feels that a woman with imagination can find creative aspects in almost any job. She certainly had done this.

After her return from college, and while her mother still lived, she and her younger, then unmarried, sister lived in the family home. It was a real center of family life. On set occasions of the year, such as Halloween and Decoration Day, the entire family gathered for an enjoyable afternoon and evening. When her younger sister married, her mother thought for a while of willing the property exclusively to her, the only remaining unmarried daughter. She wisely insisted that her mother consider the matter carefully. She equally resisted an overgenerous impulse to suggest that the mother give the property in its entirely to the brother who had the largest family and the greatest need.

She suggested eventually that her mother dispose of the property equally to all the children. When her mother died, she was able to sell her share and invest it wisely. Between her investment and her salary she has security for the future.

She has remained close to her family. The big get-togethers continue with only slight variations from the previous patterns. She rates as her closest friend a sister-in-law who is the wife of her favorite brother. She has time occasionally to spend with her nephews and nieces. She takes them to the latest Disney movies and enjoys their company.

After her mother's death, she thought for a while of sharing an apartment with someone else. She realized this would be pleasant if she and her roommate shared mutual interests. Had she been younger she most probably would have preferred the freedom of apartment living. She knew, too, that some women lived alone and liked it. But that had

had no appeal for her.

She decided to move to a residence for professional women. She has never regretted this choice. Here she has the companionship of many women of similar educational background and similar work interests. She still retains her privacy. She does not have to bother about marketing, cooking, or housework. She enjoys the religious atmosphere under which the residence carries on its program. The costs have proven reasonable, the location is convenient to her work, to church, to her creative activities. The few rules are no burden.

She takes a calm view of life. She sees that in the course of a year she will be bouncingly happy on three hundred days, down on perhaps sixty, and deep down on five or six. She realizes that these deep-down days often follow a period of tedium or tiredness or that intermediate land of half-health when a cold clings on "for the duration."

She is very careful then to limit her use of liquid refreshment of a Kentucky character. She likes an occasional "Grasshopper" but does not drink alone and never as a crutch. She takes neither a puritanical nor a bacchanalian view of drink in her own life and the lives of others.

She avoids routine, even going so far as to give away a favorite teacup every once in a while just to keep from having tea at the same time in the same cup and with the same type of tea day after day.

She is not the person to make friends widely and easily. She has a few close and dear friends. Most of these belong to her religious group.

Each year she spends a little less time on the tennis court and a little more in creative projects of a religious or welfare nature. She has never been a candidate for Miss America. She has received no award as an outstanding woman in the city. She has never been chosen one of the ten best-dressed women in the state. But her life is a full one, a creative one, and above all, a happy one. She trusts in the loving kindness of her Heavenly Father that her eternal life will be happy too.

In his role as Director of the St. Stanislaus Jesuit Museum,
Father Faherty presents the William Heithaus Award to Robert
F. Arteaga as Arteaga's grandson Bradley looks on.

This moment is for those few writers who can sell their work to Hollywood. Here Barnaby Faherty chats with Anjanette Comer on the set of <u>Guns</u> <u>for</u> <u>San</u> <u>Sebastian</u>.

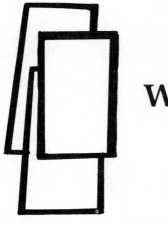

WRITER

Barnaby Faherty, the writer, is not only a prolific producer -- short fiction, historical essays, novels, meditations, prayers, histories, sermons, letters, biographies -- but also a painstaking artist. But this craft, his art, only rarely, and then very briefly, serves as the subject of his writing. He speaks of choosing names carefully, of putting strength in verbs, and of modeling after great writers, but, for the most part, when he gives advice to writers, he stresses marketing. He writes and speaks of choosing subjects according to the market. He even speaks of teaching writing by stressing sales, remembering Clarence McAuliffe's role as moderator of the St. Peter Canisius Writer's Guild. "Clarence McAuliffe insisted from the start that we would concern ourselves with marketing. He would reserve recommendations for writing to one-to-one contacts. In our meeting we spent our time relating marketing experiences and suggesting outlets to others. On the rare occasion when somebody whose interest was more in analyzing writing led the discussion, little would come from the session. Early I saw the difference in approach between the Guild concerned with marketing and the Guild concerned with writing.

A PRIEST FOR ALL REASON

I developed a negative view of public criticism, seeing that too often it proved discouraging."

Aside from marketing, Father Faherty's writing about writing directs itself toward encouraging writers: cheerleading, motivating them to keep after their writing and their marketing.

Clearly, for him, writing is a matter of doing rather than a subject to talk about. And what he does most of all is tell stories. Clearly he sees the writer as a story teller and his writing reflects this enjoyment of a good story. In the following selections we watch him as a young writer in "Beyond the Fog" looking inside a young priest with all the insecurities suffered by a young professional and we watch the secure and experienced historian turning to his craft as a writer to pull together enormous amounts of factual information to make a story about "Race Relations" clear and lively. In addition we meet two fascinating characters, Mrs. Zachstammer and Father Paul Doncoeur, each a classic underdog. We see the Kansas he knew as a young man and follow Verhaegen in the midwest; in the Christmas Novena, we are led through a re-creation of Christ's birth day. In all these pieces, as well as the Hospital prayer, Father Faherty shows the story teller's love for detail and specifics, his joy in sharing, his delight in writing. This sense of essential glee in story-telling probably accounts, to a large degree, for his success.

Beyond the Fog"
from The St. Anthony Messenger, Spring, 1945

A thin, darkly-clad man moved cautiously through the choking fog past a row of shabby riverfront houses. Though he seemed young and vigorous, he limped badly.

Now what could that fellow be up to at this hour of the morning, wondered Patrolman Heffling, as he watched the tall figure coming towards him. In the momentary flare of a match as the man lit a cigarette, the Officer noticed the lean, trembling fingers, the hard chin, a look of worry in the face. This fellow's worth watching, he concluded. From the river came the deep bass of a fog-blinded tug-boat.

Suddenly the man saw the policeman. "Oh! How are you, Officer?"

Heffling's face relaxed into a broad easy smile when he noticed the Roman collar. "Good morning, Father. Not a fit morning for man or beast, is it?" In Heffling's mouth this trite phrase carried the warmth of a novel idea.

"You're right, Officer. Only patrolmen, doctors and the clergy get out on days like this. By the way, Wharf Street will take me to the jail, won't it?"

"Five blocks straight ahead, Father," said Heffling, pointing to the river. "The main gate's around the corner. I guess you're taking Father McElroy's place." He hesitated, then continued thoughtfully, "He's been caring for the boys there close to twenty years, I guess."

"And it's only a heart attack that's keeping him away this morning." The priest smiled. "I'm afraid I'll have a hard time filling his shoes."

The patrolman pulled the rim of his cap lower to shield his eyes from the mist. "Well, it won't be easy, Father. That Jimmy What's-His-Name takes the long walk in a few hours. I hope you bring him around. He's a tough customer, mind you."

"Thank you, Officer. Thank you."

As he pushed his way into the fog, uneasy thoughts kept running through Father Dave Scanlon's mind. Usually confident, he felt appalled at the task ahead of him. For a moment he listened to the wail of a patrol siren, then pushed back the left sleeve of his coat and looked at his watch. Five to six!

Three hours and it's over for Jimmy Litwhile, he thought. Of all days for Father McElroy to get sick. A rush of cold air from the river sent a chill through him. If saintly little Father McElroy couldn't bring Jimmy around, how am I supposed to do it!

He recalled the veteran chaplain's warning to him, "My toughest case in seventeen years! Not the slightest sign of repentance."

He felt helpless, like a rookie substituting for a star-hitter in the clutch. A cold feeling gripped his stomach. This job's for keeps. No extra innings. He stopped and looked slowly about. The fog seemed to press upon him. He could see nothing. If I fail, the game's over!

He rubbed his throat with his left thumb. The skin was damp. Sometimes you have to stand between life and eternity and you haven't got what it takes. A dray horse clop-clopped on the cobblestones a few yards ahead of him.

With a jerky motion he rubbed his cigarette out against the wall of a building. This is down Father McElroy's alley, not mine!

His thoughts turned for a moment to a morning off a New Guinea beachhead. Same fog. You could have clipped it with a bayonet. But warmer. And the same uncertainty. You couldn't tell what was beyond...

He flicked the dead cigarette into the gutter. God seemed to be pushing souls into my hands out there. I knew they'd come around. Just so I'd be on hand when they did. That was the type of work I felt I was ordained for.

His steps were slow.

Sure, some were tough at the start. Wanted no truck with Holy Joes. But sooner or later God would bring them across. I knew I was winning then.

At that moment Father Scanlon caught his first glimpse of the jail through the fog. The huge outer wall seemed to lean over him ominously, recalling the hulk of an LST-boat that loomed suddenly alongside his landing barge the clammy morning of the New Guinea invasion. The tugboat on the river still sent out its frantic warnings.

That was the day Joe Carlson died. Hard as limestone. Cocksure of himself. "I don't need any priest," he had boasted. No, not until his first battle. The priest smiled a lot. Battles are God's pay-off, too. I did more good in five minutes there, then I'll do the rest of my life at home.

He re-pictured the scene. Shelltorn palms, blasted pill-boxes, heaving sand. Then the sharp cry of pain off to his left. The confession. . . And Joe was gone!

It would always remain a vivid memory, the last confession he had heard in battle. A sniper's bullet pierced his leg a few minutes later, sending him back to base hospital and eventually to civilian life.

He jay-walked to the north side of the street. The

deep-toned bell of the old cathedral seemed to come from
all directions. I doubt if many will get out for Mass
this morning, he concluded mechanically, tightening his
raincoat to ward off the penetrating mist.

He entered the jail-yard and crossed the cobblestones to the main gate. In a few moments he was walking
in step with the warden down the narrow oppressive cell
block. Their footsteps re-echoed through the hollow
corridors. The unpleasant ordor of disinfectant seemed
everywhere.

"Tough kid, that Jimmy Litwhile," the warden ob-
served.

"Yes, I've heard Father McElroy speak of him," the
priest answered. He recalled the veteran chaplain's
words. "My toughest case in seventeen years. Reformatory for theft at fourteen. County jail for a dozen
highway robberies at eighteen. Now death for robbery and
steel-cold murder! And no sign of repentance."

The door of the death chamber stood open on the
left. As they passed, the priest noticed at the other
end the cold, dark chair of death.

"O God! Help me!" he prayed.

Suddenly the warden turned a corner and unlocked a
cell door. "There he is, Father. Good luck." The
warden's voice had the dull sound of a counterfeit nic-
kel.

In front of the priest on the edge of a high cot sat
Jimmy Litwhile, dangling his long legs to the floor. He
was tow-headed, sturdy, with a slight roundness in his
wide shoulders. Gee, this fellow looks familiar, Father
Scanlan thought. Just like dozens of boys I met on the
"Canal" or Pelelieu. At that moment Jimmy raised his
eyes. Father Scanlan stopped comparing.

Most of the others had soft eyes, eyes full of fear
for the next day's battle, but ready to face death.
These were hard eyes, a frozen gray like winter clouds
that peer down on a world unconcerned.

"Good morning, Jim," the priest stammered. "I'm
Father Scanlan. Father McElroy can't be here this morning. He had a heart attack last night."

Jimmy stated straight at the priest, obviously unin-
terested. Father Scanlan reached in his side pocket for
his cigarettes. They weren't there. With a fidgety motion he felt his other pockets. At last he found them.
"Have a cigarette, Jim."

The priest tapped the top of the pack against his left index finger and offered it to the criminal.

The condemned man's hand did not move. On his face the same stare, haunted, untrusting.

Attempting to be casual, Father Scanlan lit a cigarette. He took a few nervous puffs, then laid the pack on the cot near Jimmy.

Slowly Jimmy's right hand reached along the edge of the bed towards the cigarettes. The priest pretended not to notice. Equally slowly the criminal's fingers closed on a cigarette and brought it to his lips. Father Scanlan tossed the box of matches on the bed.

As Jimmy lit the cigarette, his right eye twitched nervously. With the first deep puff, his labored breathing relaxed a little.

Should I ask him if he wants to go to confession, wondered Father Scanlan, while the two smoked in silence. Though many of the boys on Pelelieu had been away from confession for years, something about the sudden appearance of enemy grenades and the rataplanning of machine-gun fire made them want to get ready. But Jim Litwhile? . . . The priest wasn't sure.

The longer I wait, he finally concluded, the harder it will be. Haltingly, he asked, "How about saying a prayer together, Jim?"

Not a muscle of the young criminal's face stirred. The priest lowered his eyes to the floor as the feeling of helplessness again avalanched his soul. O God! It's no use. I just haven't got what it takes.

Tense moments trudged by. Suddenly the priest resovled to begin the prayer alone. Despite his injured leg, he knelt down on the cell floor.

"Rabboni, When I am dying," he began deliberately.

"How glad I shall be . . . That the lamp of my life . . . Has been burned out for Thee . . . That sorrow has darkened the pathway I trod."

All at once the priest became aware that he was not praying alone. Jimmy was kneeling beside him.

"That anguish of spirit . . . Full often was mine . . . Since anguish of spirit . . . So often was Thine!"

Jimmy's voice joined the priest.

"My cherished Rabboni . . . How glad shall I be . . . To die with the hope . . . Of a welcome from Thee."

Gosh, what could have happened? the priest wondered. But no use hesitating now! "Do you want to go to confession, Jim?"

At that moment Jimmy noticed that he still held his cigarette. Automatically he tapped it out on the framework of the bed, then leaned over, his hand supporting his forehead.

"Yes . . . I'll go."

Jimmy stammered through the long-untold story, an occasional question of the priest helping him. Then, reciting the words after the priest, he made his act of contrition. The two prayed in silence a few minutes.

The priest rose, wiping his forehead. "God has been awfully good to you."

"It was that prayer, Father," responded Jimmy, a ghost of a smile playing on his lips. He took something from the ledge above his bed. "Remember this card? I used to read it every day."

"I can't recall." said Father Scanlan, puzzled, as he reached for the frayed-edged card. It was a picture of Christ and the poem Rabboni they had just recited.

"Remember the other time we said that together, Father? After your Mass, at the Reformatory, years ago? The Company Officer made me say I was sorry for fooling around during your sermon?"

Suddenly his look of amazement disappeared. Father Scanlan smiled, as the scene of his first assignment in the priesthood returned to him. The Reformatory where he had said Mass . . . The boys in front of him during the sermon . . . The tow-headed lad by the window determined on polishing his belt buckle . . .

After Mass the C.O. had brought the boy to apologize. There had been reluctance, embarrassed uncertainty in the lad's face. The priest remembered that instead of scolding the boy he had given him a prayer card. Every detail was a vivid memory.

Father Scanlan looked again at the word Rabboni, and mechanically turned it over. On the back he read the words, "A remembrance of my ordination to the Priesthood, June 16, 1937, Reverend Charles David Scanlan."

"Hospital Prayer"

Dear Lord
who praised the ministry of healing with the words "I was sick and you visited me," Grant us the largeness of soul

to develop within the homes and hospitals under our care an agreeable atmosphere for those who are ill, a warm welcome for those who come to visit them, and a spirit of dedication for those who tend their illnesses. Bless all of us and our families, and those who work directly with the ill; take care of all who are sick, console the dying, assuage the sorrow of their dear ones; and, when our lives have run their course, bring all of us to our home with you in heaven. Amen.

"The Voice of Unshackled France"
from The Sunset Review, October, 1949

Premier Herriot was not a soldier of France during the war. Had he wallowed in the grimy trenches of Flanders, or bled in the hell box before Verdun, he could not have drawn up the document he held in his hands. But he had watched the war in the security of the Minsitry of Public Works.

His cabinet sat quietly, expectant. The Premier wanted to discuss something important. What would it be? The occupation of the Ruhr, perhaps, or the reparations, or something concerning the colonies?

"In 1902 all religious orders were exiled from France", he began, with the quiet manner of a modern electrocutioner, who pulls a switch, rather than that of a medieval hangman who wields a gory axe. "They returned at the outset of the War with Germany. It's about time they started on their travels again. Here's a draft of the proposed 'Laws on Religious Orders'. . ."

Like circular ripples expanding from a disturbance on the surface of a lake, news spread through France that monks and friars were to go. They had come back from remote mission outposts, when La Belle France needed them. That need was past. Veteran religious who had packed their grips in 1902, began to inspect the railroad timetables for convenient trains to Brussels or the coast.

But one man did not bestir himself. When the lay-brother made his rounds at the Jesuit House in Epernay to turn out the lights after night prayers, he noticed that the room of Father Paul Doncoeur was still bright.

"I guess he can't get to sleep," the Brother said to himself. "The wound he received on the Marne must be bothering him again. Those nine war medals don't seem to help now." He flicked the hall switch and went to bed.

Paul Doncoeur did not realize that the hour of re-tiring had come. He was writing an important letter -- a letter to the Premier of France! He finished the lengthy missive, and signed his name. Then picked up the paper and began to read:

"I lived twelve years in exile, from the age of twenty-one to thirty-four, the best part of a man's life. But on August 2, 1914, I was on my knees before my Super-ior. 'Tomorrow means war', I said. My Superior embraced me and gave me his blessing."

Father Doncoeur paused, looked into the blackness beyond the window, and after a moment's hesitation, went on.

"On crazy trains, without mobilization orders, with-out military booklet, I followed the guns to Verdun. On August 20th at dawn, before the renewal of fighting, I went out to look for the wounded of the 115th, and ad-vanced beyond the outposts, when suddenly I was sur-rounded by the crackling of twenty rifles. I saw my com-rade stretched full-length on the ground beside me with his head crushed. The German post was thirty steps away. I felt at that moment that my heart was protecting my whole country. Never did I breathe the air of France with such pride, nor tread her soil with such assurance.

"How I was not killed at that time, nor twenty times since, I do not understand. I still have in my body a fragment of shell received on the Marne. After being de-mobilized, I committed the crime of staying at home. And now you show me the door?"

He spat the last words from close-set teeth! A pause --

"You must be joking M. Herriot -- But one does not joke over these things.

"Never during fifty months did you seek me out either at Tracy-le-Cal, or at the Fort at Vaux, or at Tahure. I did not see you anywhere, talking about your 'Laws on Religious Orders', and yet you dare to produce them today!

"Can you think of such a thing?

"Neither I, nor any other man, nor any woman will take the road to Belgium again. Never. Nous n'irons pas!

"You may do as you please. You may take our houses. You may open your prisons. But leave as we did in 1902?

63

Never!

"Today, we have more blood in our veins, and then, you see as soldiers of Verdun we were in the right place to learn how to hold our ground! We were not afraid of bullets, or gas, or the bravest soldiers of the Guards. We shall not be afraid of political slackers.

"And now I tell you why we shall not leave. Dispossession does not frighten us. We own neither roof nor field. Jesus Christ awaits us everywhere and suffices unto the end of the world.

"But we shall not leave because we do not want a Belgian or an Englishman or an American or a Chinaman or a German to meet us far from home some day, and ask us certain questions, to which we would be forced to reply with downcast head: 'France has driven us out.'"

"For the honor of France -- do you understand that word as I do? - for the honor of France we shall never again say such a thing to a foreigner. Therefore, we shall stay, every one of us. We swear it on the graves of the dead. Nous n'irons pas!"

Father Doncoeur slumped into his chair, and fell into a troubled sleep.

La Semaine of Epernay carried the letter on its editorial page the following evening. The Rheims Matin featured it the next morning. On the third day Parisians read it on the front page of Parid Soir. Premier Herriot was one of these Parisians.

There was another meeting of the cabinet. All were expectant and less quiet as they took their place. Excited gesticulations accompanied widespread questions. Had the Premier read the letter of Father Doncoeur? Would he discuss the Laws on Religious as he had planned? What would he do?

"I have a matter of utmost importance to discuss with you". The Premier's words were as studied as the sentence of a judge. "It concerns the recent uprising in Morocco . . . ."

"Vignettes"
from Kansas Magazine, 1946

Autumn in St. Marys does not dazzle you with a carnival of colors as the painted Ozark Hills. And her woods differ from the Wisconsin forests where the foliage is brightly daubed like a Sauk brave in warpaint and feathers. Only sumac fires, burning brightly along the ridges, rival the brilliance of other areas. No pear-hued hard maples; few ashes in tangerine dresses; rare red or chestnut oaks, except in the distant woods along the Kaw.

No! Autumn in St. Marys is not a brief ectasy but a long, lingering second summer, when clear day follows clear day, and the steady bombardment of husked corn resounds against the bangboard of the farmer's wagon and hawks wheel lazily overhead.

It is not a brilliant sunset, but a tarrying, peaceful twilight at the close of the year.

At first you may have felt deep disappointment at not seeing the autumnal splendor you once knew. But some morning you stand on the north ridge watching the mist rise slowly from the floor of the Kaw Valley and then you realize in your heart that this is the best autumn you have ever known.

Indian Summer Reverie

The hunter's moon dipped like a boy's sailboat behind a wave of clouds. In the semi-darkness the shocks of corn resembled rows of Kiowan tepees that once dotted these Kansas maize fields.

After leaning my gun against a walnut stump, I sat down. Reaching into my hunting jacket, I took out a yellow Calhoun County apple. The tang of autumn was in its strong taste. Rex muzzled my instep and then dropped beside my left foot, tired from the night's hunt. An owl, hooting eerily at the edge of an oak forest, added a discordant note to the peace of night.

The scene faded and I saw a picture of years ago. The smell of wood-smoke and burning leaves seemed to come from the hundreds tepees that had been a few minutes before shocks of corn. Between the wigwams my imagination pictured bronze braves dancing here and there, raising their hands regularly in silent appeal to the half-hid Queen of Night. Entranced, I watched for a long time the graceful movements of their agile bodies.

Suddenly the moon burst from the curtain of clouds. Before me no longer stood a Kiowan village but only the carefully spaced rows of shocked corn.

A PRIEST FOR ALL REASON

Nostalgia touched me with its soft, sad fingers. As I viewed the scene I knew that Indian Summer was nearing its death. Old Man Winter, the Genghis Khan of the seasons, would soon begin his inexorable march across the expanse of America, like the giant glacier that had rolled down from the North before the Coming of the White Man.

"Peter Verhaegen - Pioneer Missouri Jesuit"
from The Jesuit Bulletin,
September, 1976

Three men stand out among the pioneer Belgian missionaries who arrived in Missouri in 1823 to begin one of the most fruitful educational and religious enterprises in the history of the Midwest. Fr. Felix Van Quickenborne was director of the initial operation; Peter Jan De Smet, a seminarian at the time, was to become world famous as a missionary among the Northwest Indians. Peter Verhaegen, less known than the other two, was the strong oak of the entire operation. He not only accomplished much himself, but was responsible in great part for the ultimate success of Van Quickenborne's efforts, and for the initial venture of De Smet among the Northwest Indians.

Peter J. Verhaegen, the second Jesuit priest to be ordained in Missouri, was born in Belgium in 1800. He came to the United States at the urging of Rev. Charles Nerinckx, Belgian-born missioner who worked throughout the Midwest from his headquarters in Kentucky. During his first years in Missouri, Verhaegen continued his studies for the priesthood, taught theology to his companions in the Florissant seminary, and participated in the education of Indian boys at the short-lived St. Regis Indian School opened there in 1828.

Verhaegen was six feet in height, of robust frame, with a tendency to over-weight. In spite of his plain features, his appearance was impressive. He was to prove a typical westerner of his time, optimistic, expansive, and always ready for new enterprises. He learned English readily. He spoke and wrote it well, as his extant letters and articles attest. He read widely, and especially liked poetry, which he cited regularly. He even tried his hand on occasion at a few patriotic verses and songs.

In spite of his metallic voice and low-keyed delivery, Verhaegen soon won a fine reputation as a speaker
among all age groups and educational backgrounds. His
outgoing personality and generosity matched his large
frame. Easy of access, he could unbend with the smallest
child. He was a popular man and a loyal friend. Like so
many new arrivals in his time, he thoroughly adapted himself to American life.

Peter Verhaegen first publicly manifested his above-
average competence in a report to the Jesuit superior in
Maryland on the Indian School conducted at Florissant.
His orderly mind and his ability to discern relevant issues shine out in this remarkable appraisal. This document no doubt helped influence the superior in approving
the appointment of Fr. Verhaegen as first Jesuit president of St. Louis University.

Bishop Rosati of St. Louis had invited the Jesuit
Fathers to man the small St. Louis College which his pre-
decessor Bishop William DuBourg had begun in 1818. In
1828 the Jesuits began temporary classes at Florissant
for a small group of students while adequate buildings
were erected on a new campus at Ninth and Washington,
just then west of the St. Louis city limits. The Jesuits
began to teach there the following year. Father President Verhaegen directed the school and taught several
classes.

Verhaegen saw that the population of St. Louis was
still fluctuating. To stabilize the student body, he
sought residential students from the more settled planter
groups in French Louisiana. Taking advantage of steamboat traffic, he sent a representative of the school
south to recruit students. For the ensuing few years,
the residential students at St. Louis were chiefly from
the Bayou country.

Even though St. Louis College, like so many schools
of its time, hardly reached the high school level, Verhaegen anticipated future grown and applied for a university charter in 1832. When the state of Missouri
granted the charter in December of that year, Verhaegen
was thirty-two years and six months of age. He was to
prove St. Louis University's greatest president of the
19th Century. He was the youngest in its entire history.

One of his greatest contributions to education in
Missouri was the decision to set up a medical school. In
1835 Verhaegen proposed to the University trustees that

he be authorized to consult physicians of the city about a medical faculty. The trustees approved this recommendation. Several factors, including the panic of 1837, held back the opening of the medical department for a few years. In the fall of 1842, the College of Medicine of St. Louis University was formally opened.

In the meantime, Fr. Verhaegen left his presidency of the University to become regional director of the entire Jesuit activity in the Midwest in 1836. His first action was to bring the headquarters of this operation from the village of Florissant to the city of St. Louis. He served as president of the Board of Trustees of St. Louis University and continued his interest in the affairs of the institution. He also gave attention to the expanding problems of the entire Midwestern country.

In spite of the limited manpower available to Verhaegen as superior of the Jesuits of the mid-continent, he sent men to staff St. Charles College at Grand Coteau, Louisiana, and authorized John Elet to begin St. Xavier College in Cincinnati. The former was to become a Jesuit seminary for the entire South. The latter grew into Xavier University.

One of the truly significant decisions of Fr. Verhaegen was his response to the delegation of Indians who came from the Northwest to ask for a "Blackrobe." Volunteers were numerous from the small band of Belgian Jesuits. Verhaegen preferred his close friend, Peter Jan De Smet, for the task.

When Fr. De Smet had become ill a few years before in 1833, and had requested a reassignment to Belgium, Verhaegen proved an understanding and sympathetic friend. He had commissioned De Smet as special representative of St. Louis University in several business matters. He gave him a vote of confidence when authorities in Rome doubted that De Smet would be able to continue as a member of the Missouri Province.

After a few years in Belgium, De Smet's health had recovered sufficiently. He was able to return to Missouri. In 1840 Verhaegen sent him along the pathway untrod by white men until thirty-six years before when Lewis and Clark had moved into the Pacific Northwest. De Smet was to be a name of shining light in American History -- a successful missioner among countless tribes, a peacemaker between the United States and the Sioux, a best-selling writer of experiences in the early West.

The work he and his associates performed among the various tribes is legend.

So well did Verhaegen handle Missouri Jesuit affairs that Bishop Rosati recommended him, along with two Vincentians, for the position of coadjutor bishop of St. Louis in 1838. Rome did not act on the recommendation. When Rosati journeyed to the Eternal City in April of 1840, he appointed Verhaegen administrator of the St. Louis diocese. During these months Verhaegen spent a portion of his day at the episcopal residence on Walnut Street, and the other half on Washington Avenue, conducting the affairs of the Missouri Jesuits.

In 1843 Verhaegen finished his term as superior of the Midwestern Jesuits. For six years, from January, 1845, until 1851, he employed his talents beyond the borders of Missouri. For three years he was provincial of the Maryland Jesuits. During the next three years he directed a new college, St. Joseph's in Bardstown, Kentucky. After that he returned to Missouri to be pastor of the parish in St. Charles.

A Methodist minister, Robert Rose, and his co-author, W.B. Bryan, wrote of Verhaegen's pastoral years in their History of Pioneer Families in Missouri: "The Belgian priest left a deep impression on Protestants as well as Catholics. He was a man of superior mind and profound knowledge and of genial manners, with a kind word for all who came near him."

Verhaegen, in conclusion, stands pre-eminent among the pioneer Jesuits of the American Midwest. While Van Quickenborne founded the Jesuit Mission of Missouri, and De Smet brought it great renown, Verhaegen planted the roots of this important religious and cultural foundation deep in the soil of the mid-continent. To him it owes its permanence and its lasting achievements.

A PRIEST FOR ALL REASON

"The Incarceration of Mrs. Zachstammer"
Colorado Wonderland
prize-winning story, 1956

Like a piece of unpolished quartz in a setting made for the Hope Diamond, the collection of ugly buildings called Silver City lay in one of the most awe-inspiring canyons of the High Rockies.

The men who had come for the precious metals just before the turn of the century did not care for the looks of the buildings where they lived, or drank, or did business. So the long, narrow gulch overflowed with nondescript disharmonious constructions, piled higgledy-piggledy along the canyon walls.

At the far end, closing the valley, stood the old Church of Bishop Renaldeaux, the whole town seeming to flow from it, as from a mountain spring. Many a time the brick face of the venerable edifice must have turned a deeper red at Saturday night's skylarking along Silver City's main street.

But that was a long time ago. As inevitably as the spring sun melts the snow on the face of Placer Mountain, a bust followed the Silver City boom. The Matchless Mine closed, then the Guerra, then the Burris. The fly-by-nighters scurried out of the gulch; only a few crusted old sourdoughs would not budge.

Silver City's vigorous life slowed to a halt. Only the fact that it was the county seat prevented it from becoming a total ghost town . . .

Years went by. The Second World War came and went. Then an enterprising easterner saw new sources of silver in the high hills.

He purchased the Strand Imperial Hotel, the one handsome building in town, and restored it to its old splendor. Taking advantage of the cool summer climate, he began a music festival that caught like a mountain fire in dry timber. Cars of sightseers and all-summer guests crammed the tight canyon.

Some of the old-timers, like Mrs. Zachstammer, viewed these proceedings with yes-and-no feelings. Her combination restaurant and grocery store had been just enough to live on, and she was happy.

But with this new summer influx, she had to get extra help for three months of rush and then settle down to the quiet rest-of-the-year routine.

Short, squat Mrs. Zachstammer was as rugged and un-
changing as the canyon walls behind her store. With all
the high-toned goings-on, she still refused to paint her
storefront, or spruce up the gingham table cloths, or get
fancy menus.

Unfortunately, the new Silver City sheriff did not
fathom the woman. One bright afternoon he parked his car
down the street from Mrs. Zachstammer's restaurant.

"The Capitol crowd is getting a bit worried about
gambling up this way," Sheriff Biggs said to his companion. "Too many people coming in for the summer festiv-
ities."

"What do you plan to do?" asked his assistant, Norm
Brink.

"I'll slap a fine on Mrs. Zachstammer for keeping
slot-machines," the Sheriff cam back. "That will pacify
the boys down in the State House."

"You sure it's going to be that easy?" Brink's eyebrows lifted. "What if she refuses the fine and insists
on going to jail? If I know Mrs. Zachstammer--"

But Sheriff Biggs was already out of the car and
trying to get his five foot six, two hundred pound frame
up over the extra-high curbing to the sidewalk. Tall,
trim Brink reached the door first.

A woman tourist in khaki, hoping for the jackpot,
was putting an endless flow of nickles in the slot-
machine. A few patrons sat at one of the tables and Mrs.
Zachstammer was busy behind the counter.

"What can I do for you, Sheriff Biggs," she stated
with the menacing tone she reserved for the special
guests.

"You're under arrest, Mrs. Zachstammer, for keeping
slot-machines. It's against the law."

"With all this big-money, undercover gambling going
on over in the Strand Imperial, you come over to bother
me." And then she looked the little man straight in the
eye and went on, "I promise you, Sheriff Biggs, you'll be
sorry."

"The fine is one hundred dollars," and then as an
unnecessary afterthought, "or thirty days in jail."

"I'll take the jail," she shot back defiantly.

Brink looked at Biggs with a wry smile. . .

The Silver City jail was small, with two cells
behind an office -- and little else.

"Get me a Bible," Mrs. Zachstammer demanded as the

sheriff locked the cell door behind her.

As the Sheriff paid no heed to her request, Mrs. Zachstammer went on, "You cannot deprive a citizen of religious consolation. And after all, I always wanted to read the Bible and never had the time before."

"Who's got a Bible in this town, anyway?"

"Nobody here, but the pastor over in White Plume has one. Go over and borrow his. I demand my constitutional right of freedom of religion."

"That's too far!"

"Sheriff Biggs, either I get my Bible or --".

But the Sheriff had enough. He slammed the door viciously and Mrs. Zachstammer sat down on the cell cot to relax. "Yes, I always wanted to read the Bible and never had a chance . . ."

It was six-thirty when the Sheriff returned from White Plume with the Bible. "When am I going to get my dinner?" shouted Mrs. Zachstammer, as she took the Bible without even a "thank-you."

"Yeh Gods!" Biggs said under his breath, "I never thought of that!"

"There're lots of things you never thought of," Brinks answered.

Most of the townfolk and a good number of the visitors had heard of Mrs. Zachstammer's plight and lined the sidewalk as the Sheriff escorted her to her own restaurant for her evening meal. It was more a triumphal procession . . .

"You're not leaving me in this hole all by myself?" Mrs. Zachstammer asked, as the Sheriff turned out the lights at ten and started toward the door.

"You sleep in that other cell, or I'll shout loud enough to keep everybody in Silver City awake. And, anyway, it's against the law of the state for a sheriff to leave the jail overnight while a prisoner is locked up." . . . "Wake up, Sheriff. Wake up." Mrs. Zachstammer's voice was as loud and insistent at six in the morning as it has been at ten the night before.

Sheriff Biggs opened his eyes. "What's the trouble?"

"Time for church. Hurry up."

"But I never go to church."

"Well, you're going this morning, because I'm the only person in Uncompaghre County who can play the organ."

72

"O, you go alone. Let me sleep."

"Nothing doing. It's against the law. You can't let a dangerous prisoner roan around free."

"Aw, I'll deputize the choir master to watch you."

"No, you can't. I've got to play also for the Methodists at ten and the Episcopals at eleven."

By the time Mrs. Zachstammer returned from the services, Sheriff Biggs was all ready to admit he was licked. "I'll just tell her that she's free to go home," he said to Brink. "I known when I've had enough."

"But what if Mrs. Zachstammer refuses?"

"Here I am, Sheriff," she boomed. "Back in my humble little home."

"Mrs. Zachstammer," the Sheriff began apologetically, "I realize I made a mistake yesterday. You're a God-fearing, church-going woman, I'm going to let you free."

"O no you don't," she came back, her undershot jaw looking like Gibraltar. "You said thirty days and thirty days it will be." . . .

By the middle of the week, the imprisonment of Mrs. Zachstammer was state-wide news. She made the headlines in the metropolitan dailies. A special bulletin each day announced the latest news from Silver City and told how many days she had yet to serve. Even the size of the Governor's latest trout-catch dropped back to the second page.

By the end of the month Sheriff Biggs had wished three hundred and forty times over that he had died in the Battle of the Bulge, or drowned at sea, or succumbed in the last winter's avalanche on the Million Dollar Highway. But even thirty days finally ended and Sheriff Biggs relaxed for the first time in a month.

"Gee, it feels good to light your pipe, and know that the mad woman is gone."

Just then a young fellow came to the door. "Here's a letter for you, Sheriff. The postman asked me to bring it over."

"Zachstammer again," the Sheriff spat out the words, as he looked at the envelope.

He tore it open. It was a bill from the Zachstammer Restaurant. "For ninety meals, served to a prisoner in the Silver City jail . . . $230.29.

"O Holy Night"
from Christmas Novena

Liturgical reflection: O King of Gentiles and the Desired of all, you are the cornerstone that binds two into one: Come and save poor man whom you fashioned out of clay.

Meditation: Go back in spirit across time and space to a night almost two thousand years ago. Travel far across the world in imagination to a Judean hillside. There a group of shepherds huddle together before a small fire, wrapped in rough blankets. In the valley below are the sheep they guard. To the north, six miles away lies the capital city of Jerusalem. Across a hill to the east is Bethlehem, the city of David.

Imagine yourself joining unseen that group at the fire. Watch them on this night of nights. Listen to the words they say. A young shepherd is speaking.

"What an awful night to have to guard these silly sheep," he begins. "Just when friends and relatives have come down for the census."

There is a moment's silence, and then a veteran voice answers, "Yes, it is so. Tonight is hard. But as we go through life, we learn that these difficulties are part of God's plan. It might be that He wants us to be on this hillside tonight."

"Maybe so," comes back the younger man. "But still I would just as soon be in Bethlehem."

The night air is crisp. You draw your coat tightly around your shoulders. The smell of woodsmoke permeates the atmosphere. A shepherd dog nuzzles your instep. Suddenly he stirs. His back bristles. The shepherds jump to attention.

"Quiet," one of them says.

Then there is a flash of light and the shepherds fall back. A heavenly spirit stands before them. They tremble.

"Do not be afraid," the spirit says. And his voice is sweet as the song of the lark, yet strong as the rush of the River Jordan. "Behold I bring you good news of great joy which shall be to all the people; for there has been born to you today in the town of David a Savior who is Christ the Lord. And this shall be a sign to you; you will find an infant wrapped in swaddling clothes and laid in a manger."

Slowly the vision fades before your eyes, but the shepherds remain transfixed, as if frozen to the ground. Then the old man's voice breaks the silence, "Well, why are we waiting?"

"Sure," came back a young companion, "Let us go over to Bethlehem and see this thing that has come to pass, which the Lord has made known to us." They rush across the hillside. It is hard to keep up with them.

You follow them, but your breath comes a bit heavy now. They push on to the stable and through the door. Suddenly the men before you are on their knees. You kneel too. There is the Child with his Mother.

"Glory to God in the Highest." Your heart sings the same song God's messengers sang a short time before. "Hosanna to the Lord God of Israel."

As you kneel there in spirit you realize that He alone, the Infant in the Manger, the God-Man sent from the heavenly Father, yes, He alone can save the world, save it from sin, save it from self-destruction, save it from the chaos into which it is plunging. You realize that all mankind must kneel as you do at the feet of the Infant King. Otherwise there is no hope! For He is the way, the truth, and the Life.

Finally you rise, and back slowly out of the cave. You look up. Overhead the most brilliant star you have ever seen shines in a black velvet sky. In your heart is love and gratitude.

Prayer: Grant, we beseech you, O almighty God, that the coming festival of your Son may both bring us healing in the present life and give us rewards that are eternal. Through Christ Our Lord. Amen.

from The Saint Louis Portrait

Social observers find it somewhat amazing that Saint Louis alone of the major U.S. cities did not have a riot either in the long, hot summer of 1967 or in Holy Week of 1968, when an assassin cut down Martin Luther King in Memphis. No complete study has analyzed why, but certain factors can be considered.

First, of course, was the basic conservatism of the old-line black families that reflected in great part the heritage of the city. Many of these matched white families in their loyalty to the city and the area.

Even before World War I, the Argus newspaper had been reporting events of interest in the black community, promoting equal opportunity and working to improve education. In 1926, the American gave area blacks a second voice in print.

By the 1930's, blacks had organized their community into a strong and effective political force under the leadership of Committeeman Jordan Chambers. Voting as a block, the community had a strong say in elections, giving Chambers a powerful bargaining tool to secure patronage jobs for black Saint Louisans.

Attorney Homer G. Phillips fought influential and reluctant forces in the city to open a hospital where black doctors could practice and black patients could receive adequate care. Once opened, the initial hospital soon proved not only necessary but inadequate. The fight went on. A ten year battle, ending in 1933, saw the building of much more elaborate facilities, the current Homer G. Phillips at 2601 Whittier. The Sisters of St. Mary opened their infirmary on Papin to blacks in 1933 and began a school for black nurses, who took three of their courses at Saint Louis University.

Less than a decade later, in 1944, Saint Louis University was the pioneer among former slave state universities in integrating its faculty and student body -three years before President Truman's Commission on Higher Education recommended this step for the entire nation. Saint Louis University high school, the oldest high school in the West, followed in 1946, the first high school in Missouri to integrate.

Archbishop Ritter moved the entire city forward on the racial question in 1947 by integrating all the Catholic schools of the city, seven years before the U.S. Supreme Court pushed public schools off dead center. He planned Cardinal Glennon Memorial Hospital to provide for all children, regardless of race, religion or national origin. He called for an integrated staff.

Blacks traditionally have played an important role in the cultural life of Saint Louis. Scott Joplin played there. Alabama-born W.C. Handy wrote the song "Saint Louis Blues." Singleton Palmer and his "Dixieland Six" and songstress Jeannie Trevor kept alive the city's jazz tradition. On the operatic level, Grace Bumbry leaped from the Sumner High Glee Club to international acclaim.

Sometimes an external circumstance gave the extra push needed for better relationships. Such was an incident in professional basketball that Sports Illustrated described at length in the late 1950s, when the Saint Louis Hawks won the world's championship. The story told about Bill Russell, star center on the Celtics, a black athlete, who came in by plane late the evening before the sixth and what proved to be the final game. Coach Red Auerbach and three white stars, Bob Cousy, Tom Heinsohn, and Bill Sharman, waited for Russell to arrive, before going out to eat. When the center arrived, the five men crossed the street to a restaurant. It served whites only. They tried the hamburger shop on the corner. Again, Russell could not gain entrance. The Celtics returned to the Jefferson Hotel. At that very time, ticketless fans would have given a hundred dollars for a ticket to see those same men play. But one of them could not buy a hamburger.

Interestingly, when the Aldermanic council next voted on the issue -- after the appearance of the Sports Illustrated article -- the open-access ordinance won the needed votes and became a law.

Many Saint Louis religious leaders had participated in such demonstrations as the Selma March and had expressed their concern for improvement. The city government had defused possible excessive reaction by slowly and sometimes reluctantly making concessions; but these concessions came steadily. Saint Louis blacks always saw a promise of better times.

The city gradually called more and more competent blacks into positions of administration. William Clay of Saint Louis became the first Missouri black in the U.S. House of Representatives. Judge Theodore McMillian served on the Missouri Court of Appeals. As blacks showed their capacities in political office, and, above all, their concern to serve the whole community, the entire situation bettered itself.

In the summer of 1967, at the very time when tensions were extremely high in other areas, Bob Gibson, Lou Brock, and Curt Flood were leading the Saint Louis Cardinals, along with Orlando Cepeda, Roger Maris, and Steve Carlton, to a world championship. On some of those warm summer nights, Bob Gibson's fast ball seemed much more immediately important than the possibility of riots and burnings. In short, a complexus of long-standing policies and fortunate circumstances of the times helped Saint Louis over that difficult period.

Saint Louis may have moved slowly most of the time, but it was moving, and the sincere blacks and more progressive whites realized that. They felt further that it was their city, for better or for worse, and it was steadily getting better.

One of St. Louis' major attractions: the Great Cathedral.
Father Faherty stands at the Bronze Gates, a gift from the
Austro-Hungarian exhibit at the St. Louis World's Fair.

Barnaby Faherty doesn't just write about athletics. Here he competes in a downhill ski race in Colorado.

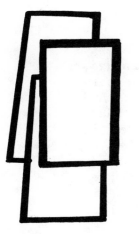

ATHLETICS

The four following sections contain selections centered around what seems to be Father Faherty's favorite subjects, areas on which his writing seems to focus most intensely: athletics, St. Louis, people, and the Church.

The first, athletics, represents a long-standing interest with Father Faherty. As a young boy, like most young American boys of his time, he loved whatever sports he had time and chance to play -- soccer, baseball, gymnastics, swimming. As a young man, he coached basketball, football, and track. Like most of his peers, he continues his interest -- reading about, listening to and watching on TV and in person football, hockey, baseball, soccer -- whatever. And, he talks, discusses, argues sports any time a partner stands ready. Unlike most of his contemporaries, however, Barnaby Faherty has continued as a participant in athletics on into his adult years. Skiing, swimming, tennis -- he plays them all today.

In the following selections, we read about some of his favorite sports as he writes from the perspective of priest and historian. The first, "Easter Sunrise at the Ski Chapel," published in the secular magazine, Colorado Wonderland, contains one of the more attractive and concrete images of Heaven ever to occur in secular or religious writings. The historian in Barnaby Faherty emerges as he traces the chapel to its beginnings, the writer comes out in the sketches of the persons most prominent among the communicants. And the reader knows that only a priest could produce this sermonette. But through it all, under it all, embracing its vision -- here stands a skier.

In "Slalom at Climax," we find an extraordinary picture of competitive skiing as experienced by a competition skier. Here he transports his reader to the race through stunning detail; here he places his reader in the midst of the bantering athletes as only one who has been there could do.

As much as he clearly loves sports, Faherty sees them in a clear perspective. On the one hand, they do not deserve center stage throughout one's life. As wonderful as winning a football game might seem - especially to a not quite nineteen year-old hero -- a game remains a game, "not the most important thing in life." On the other hand sports can teach about life. Don Coryell -- famous for his single-minded commitment to football -- provides Father Faherty with advice about life, a way to approach life's worries like a confident and skillful sports person.

The two final selections, "Chip Off the Old Bat" and "The Cochems' Years," demonstrate Father Faherty's chief strength as a historian the ability to pull together details into one whole. Remarkably, they total something just over a couple thousand words. And in that short space lies a rare kind of factual density -- a kind easy to comprehend. Barnaby Faherty's ability to synthesize, to draw material together makes this richness go unnoticed.

In "Cochem's Years" from Better the Dream, he shows his loyalty to his school, using his abilities as writer-historian to toot that school's horn a bit. He carefully substantiates, in this piece, the kind of importance athletics played in the history of the school and in the lives of its athletes. In "Chip Off the Old Bat" the richness of the details form a strong supporting fabric for a story that will bring back warm memories for anyone who played sports and read about them -- once, some time ago.

"Easter Sunrise at the Ski Chapel"
Colorado Wonderland, April 1956

"He is risen as he said! Alleluia!"

"This is the day that the Lord hath made. Rejoice and be glad therein."

These words of Easter morning will ring through vast cathedrals and magnificent temples where the worshippers reach the thousands.

They will ring with less solemnity but equal sincerity in the little ski chapel of Our Lady of the Way, near Fraser, Colorado.

Here in the midst of such popular ski areas as Winter Park and Berthoud Pass stands the spiritual center of hundreds of skiers. For a brief hour they will forget the powdered snow of "Mulligan's Mile" or the Berthoud Face and turn their thoughts to the great day in Jerusalem, when the crucified Christ rose from the tomb and appeared to His Apostles and the holy women of Galilee.

Easter vacation offers a splendid opportunity for countless skiers of other parts of the country to come to Colorado for a taste of excellent spring skiing. Many choose the Berthoud Pass-Winter Park area precisely because they can attend Mass on Easter at the ski chapel.

Here they will kneel alongside many old-time mountaineers: ruddy-faced Dick Mulligan, who operated the T-Bar on the Beginners Slope at Winter Park; rancher Nicholas Stadelman, whose son always assists as server at the eight o'clock Mass; Mark Lee, who insists that skiing is not a sport, but "a disease of the most dangerous kind"; and "Whispering Pete" Karpen, sexton of the Chapel, who welcomes all visitors with a voice that can be heard from Berthoud Pass to Grand Lake, and whose vigorous gestures generally leave bruises on the arms of all his hearers.

Situated on the side of the great national highway U.S. 40, the Chapel of Our Lady of the Way took its name from an ancient shrine of the same name in Rome, the center of Christendom.

Several summers ago Father Walter Luebke, S.J., Physics Professor at Regis College in Denver, reconstructed the first floor rooms of the old Cozens Ranch House, the oldest ranch west of the Continental Divide in Northwest Colorado. By removing two inside partitions, the priest handyman was able to provide an L-shaped room for fifty or sixty worshippers. During the summer it serves as the spiritual rendezvous of guest ranchers in the neighborhood. It is staffed by Jesuit Fathers from Regis High School and College who offer the eight and nine o'clock Masses all year around.

As the chapel bell summons the skiers for the Easter services, the newly-fallen snow glistens like a jeweler's window, the scent of Western Yellow Pine invigorates the still air, the sun lifts a happy eye over the Continental Divide and the entire countryside seems to wrap one it its calm and comforting embrace.

In the midst of such grandeur it is not hard to feel the uplifting message of Easter: that as Christ rose so we shall one day rise, that death does not confine us to a lifeless tomb on earth, but awakens us to the eternal winter wonderland, where there will always be fresh powder snow, and the T-Bars will never break down.

"Slalom at Climax"
from Queen's Work, December, 1959

When Jim Soraghan skied a slalom course, he looked as if he were going to knock the hill down. Form did not matter with him. He leaped forward, like a snow plow eyeing a fresh drift.

He was set up like a snow plow, in fact, square and broad all the way up and down, and not too tall.

He was no stylist, dancing through the gates. He simply went straight ahead with all the speed and force he could muster -- as he did everything else, whether it was experimenting in the "phys lab" at the college, or arguing with his fellows -- he always won but never on the strength of logic or argument --, or driving a bull-dozer during the summer months. That guy doesn't need a bull-dozer, people often remarked.

Despite three falls he had finished only four seconds off the pace in the controlled downhill that morning. Had he not fallen, he would have won easily.

But he had fallen, and finished sixth, -- the captain of the team, the front runner, the man who should have been sure as the sunrise on Mount Massive. Only Bob Koborvec's great third place time had kept the Regis Rangers from falling out of contention.

And now the slalom was about to start. The skiers assembled on top of Mt. Carson, overlooking Fremont Pass and the hugh gash in the far basin, above the famed Climax Molybdenum plant.

The sun was bright and warm, the snow perfect. Though

84

the starting gate was above timberline, the vigorous aroma of pines filled the atmosphere.

The four teams, pace-setting Aggies, Mines, State and Regis, clustered like small groups of junipers on the mountain side.

Soraghan poled to the Regis group.

"Let's really roar down the hill this time," he began.

"That's why we lost the downhill, Soraghan. You take too many chances." The other three skiers looked in surprise at McCabe, the speaker. "We have to finish four men without a fall," he continued unhesitatingly. "That's what wins these races."

His teammates looked from McCabe to Soraghan. Cautious people did not walk in the way of snow plows. And McCabe was cautious, -- overly so, in fact. He was short and chubby, like a horn player in a college band. If he blew over, he would, like Humpty Dumpty, probably not roll back up again.

So thought point-blank Soraghan. "The trouble with you, McCabe, is that you haven't got any guts."

The little fat fellow did not melt into the snow. He did not roll dead down the mountain side. He looked squarely at the bridge of Soraghan's big nose and came back, "The trouble with you, Soraghan, is that you havent's got any brains."

McCabe's right, I thought as I poled toward the starting gate. Outstanding individuals can win medals while their team loses. I recalled the time that Regis won eight medals in a four-event meet, while Aggies took only three, but won the team trophy.

I took off my skis, set them upright into the deep snow and checked the field telephone. "Ready below?"

"Amost ready!" came the voice of Dr. Oliver of Aggies, who always kept time at our small college meets. "Prof" Baton of Mines was scorer, and I started the races.

Each contestant would be timed for two runs, the racer with the best combined times would win the gold medal. The team trophy would be decided on combined times, too, -- the combined times of the best four racers from each school.

"Fore-runners ready," I called to the skiers on the hillside. Both fore-runners who would try the course before the contestants were experienced racers, at the time ski instructors at neighborhing Camp Hale.

"We're ready up here" I repeated into the telephone as the front skier pointed his skis through the gates, and toed the starting line.

"Five-four," I began in unison with Dr. Oliver on the other end of the line. "Three-two-one-go." The fore-runner sped toward the bamboo poles just above timber-line which formed the first gate. The course then plunged down a forty-foot wide gap in the forest of conifers.

Every racer watched how the fore-runner zig-zagged through each gate. It was important to plan the exact maneuvering. The rules allow no contestant to pre-run a slalom.

The course was difficult because of several "tight" gates, but not dangerous. The contour of the hill made the second gate a tricky one. Three or four simple gates came next. Then at the steepest part of the hill the fore-runner reached the "flush" -- three gates set so that he had to weave like a sports car taking a double switchback on a mountain highway.

Through the flush he plunged on toward an H, an arrangement in which the first and third gates faced open to the oncoming skier, while the middle gate was at a right angle to its fellows.

Below this the fore-runner turned abruptly to the left behind a group of evergreens and disappeared towards the finish line.

Those of us on the top of the hill could only guess what went on below this point, but the tough part of the race was over by that time save for a slight dip near the bottom...

After the second fore-runner started down I called the names of the first four racers: Simduke of Aggies, Weiss of Mines, Soraghan of Regis and Gifford of State. All four tough competitors, I knew. Simduke was the man to beat.

Tall and friendly, with curly brown hair, he readied himself at the starting gate. Perfect form dated back to his high school days at Aspen. Few collegiate skiers could match him in the slalom.

"Simduke ready," I called. Then in unison with Dr. Oliver, I chanted rhythmically, "Five-Four-Three-Two-One-Go."

The "Duke" poled rapidly to the first gate, swung sharply to the left and then began his graceful weave through the intricate course. No flaw or falter marked his progress. It was as beautiful as a ballet.

I kept my ear to the telephone and heard Dr. Oliver call out: "Simduke of Aggies -- Forty one-two!"

Weiss of Mines followed. Shorter and more compactly built, he rivaled the "Duke" in speed but not in grace. His

86

time was Forty-one-four.

Soraghan bulled his way to the starting gate. Leaping away at the word "Go," he was moving much faster than the first two men by the time he reached the second gate. He continued to pick up speed through the next three easy ones.

"Too fast for the flush," someone behind me said.

Just at that moment Soraghan tried to turn sharply into the tight gate. He slipped by the lower bamboo pole, and fell. Instantaneously he was up but he lost valuable seconds climbing the hill a few steps to make the gate.

A little more cautious now, he took the "H" nicely, swung to the left, and finished the course without further mishap.

"Forty-five flat," came the unimpressed voice of Dr. Oliver over the phone.

Gifford of State followed with a forty-three-eight.

"Bruno of Aggies, Thorgard of Mines, Korbovec of Regis and Schule of State," I called.

"That sounds like a UN General assembly meeting" someone remarked, but most of the racers were too tense to laugh.

All four finished well off the pace, though Thorgard was faster than Soraghan.

Two other racers followed. And then came McCabe. How will he do? I wondered.

"McCabe ready -- Five-Four-Three-Two-One-Go."

He started easily, smoothly, with no wasted motion, but -- it seemed -- almost too slow. He roly-polyed his way through the tricky gates, then picked up speed imperceptibly. Few realized how fast he was going as he turned behind the evergreens. He never seemed to hurry.

Surprise dominated Dr. Oliver's voice, as he announced: "McCabe - Forty three-six."

He's got third place for the first run, I thought with a grin. I wonder what Soraghan will say.

The last racers did not change the pattern. Simduke of Aggies was first, Weiss of Mines second, McCabe of Regis third, Gifford of State fourt, Thorgard of Mines fifth and Soraghan of Regis sixth.

By this time the early racers reached the top of the hill ready for their second run.

The sun had passed its zenith of noon-day heat. The interval gave me time to realize how cold it was getting. I jumped up and down in the snow to warm my feet. Soraghan threw his parka to me as he stripped down for the final run.

I took my cap and sun glasses off and slipped the parka

over my shoulders. I replaced the glasses and cap and slung the hood over my head, tieing it securely.

The course was icing a bit. They won't go quite as fast this time, -- if they're smart, I concluded.

It proved an accurate surmise.

Simduke moved as gracefully as a spruce tree swaying in a February wind, but not quite as rapidly as before. His time was forty three-five.

Weiss raced cautiously, too, finished in forty-three-eight.

Just as Soraghan toed the starting gate, McCabe reached the top of the hill. A big round laugh overflowed his full face.

Soraghan was as silent as the top of Shavano Peak off to the South.

The timers were ready. I gave the signal.

Soraghan tested the snow on the first turn. Realizing its icyness he swung in a wide arc toward the second gate. He sped through the next three then side-slipped to slow down. He eased his way through the flush standing up.

With the tough part of the race over, he opened up as he approached the H, and continued to accelerate as he swung out of sight behing the coninfers.

Surprise again marked Dr. Oliver's voice as he shouted: "Forty one-eight." Nice going Jimmy, I thought to myself.

Gifford followed with another forty three-eight, an identical run with his first, despite changed snow conditions.

Thorgard also duplicated his first race, but McCabe was a second slower...

The other racers did not change the pattern of individual stars, but Regis' other racers, Korbovec and Donnelly, both had good times.

Before the last racers finished, the sun had completely lost its mid-day warmth and the thermometer went down like a racer going down an open mountain side.

I put on my skis, adjusted the bindings, and started down the hillside after the racers. Stiff from the cold, I took a very leisurely pace.

By the time I reached bottom, the scores were tabulated and "Prof" Baton began to announce the results: "Simduke of Aggies first, Weiss of Mines second, Soraghan of Regis third, Gifford of State fourth, Thorgard of Mines fifth, McCabe of Regis sixth, Schulz of CC seventh, Bruno of Aggies, eighth, Korbovec of Regis ninth, Donnelly of Regis tenth...

"First team place in the slalom goes to Regis with a third, sixth, ninth and tenth."

As a shout went up, "Prof" went on: "Those Regis fellows sure get up fast when they fall."

"Some of them have to learn not to fall, 'Prof'," McCabe ventured. "But we have hopes. Even Soraghan finally showed some small semblance of a brain."

All skiers tensed as they looked at Soraghan's grim visage. His bulldozing features relaxed, and his voice came with a grin. "Below that flush even McCabe skied as if he had some guts."

"Chronic Loser -- Or Consistent Winner?"
Radio Talk

Christ died for our sins -- yet we're gloomy.
Christ rose from the dead - and still were glum!
Christ came to bring peace to men of good will. Yet the newspapers tell us of nothing but wars, murders, rapes and robberies -- even though most men seem to try to do good. Few of us can remember when everyone seemed so glum, depressed, wondering, directionless. The government seems overwhelmed by problems at home. The state department officials rush around from nation to nation trying to hold the world together. The goals of the Ecologists run counter to those of the profiteers who cater to the demands of a people continually seeking material comforts. Our spiritual leaders offer us only the negative advice of "living patiently from day to day." They seem incapable of showing us how to win the world for Christ and so rush to diversions of all kinds, not to revivify our spirit but to forget realities.

Strangely, within all this glum world around us, certain men are able to cope with their own small areas of life and handle them effectively. They give true leadership, albeit in a restricted area. Perhaps, by listening to such men we can learn a little about straightening out our attitudes.

Just yesterday I read the recommendations of one of our professional coaches. He took a few all-around athletes, several players with specialized skills, a group of castoffs and presumed-to-be misfits, and built a champion team in a short time. His ideas on positive thinking, we may be able to transfer to our personal lives. Here are some of his guide-lines to help his men reach their full potential: "Some men consistently win, and other men with equal or more ability are chronic losers..."

"Refrain from associating with chronic complainers. Stay away from people who blame others and always have an excuse for their own failure... Most important: you are the only person who can change your own behavior, attitudes and habits. All of us are capable of improving ourselves. So don't wait--act now... Develop your strength and endurance so you can carry your work to its conclusion. Consider each setback as merely a delay, a challenge to be overcome. Develop the stability to overcome the stickyness, the irritations, the frustrations of any unpleasant situation. The difference between losing and winning often depends on whether you do the little extra things. Everyone can't be an All Pro, but everyone can work with spirit, play up to his maximum potential, develop self-respect and earn the respect of others."

Think over these suggestions. Pray for, but avoid the complainers, the people who always blame others for their troubles, the chronic losers -- the people who don't want to succeed but merely to have an excuse for failing. Have a clear cut goal in life. Expect setbacks, and accept them but merely as delays on your road. If you have a negative outlook, change your own behavior, attitudes, habits. Improve yourself now! Develop your strength and endurance, a stability to overcome temporary unpleasant situations. Do the little things that make the difference between success and failure and remember often little things are the key. Respect yourself and others will respect you.

As you heard these words, you saw how readily they apply to all aspects of life. I'm sure, too, that you saw that these suggestions will make your life happier and thus indirectly help you spiritually.

"Chip off the Old Bat"
from Queen's Work, October, 1957

Forty thousand fans choked momentarily as the announcer blared out over the P.A., "George Sully batting for Zales." Old George Sully, the veteran, was coming in to pinch-hit against his rookie son, Tom, who had just taken the mound.

Two were out in the last of the ninth. Runners stood on second and third. The score was one to nothing. It was the seventh game of the World Series, and last bats for the home team.

Even the October sun seemed to grow warmer with the

tension.

For nineteen years George had looked forward to the day when he and his son might play in the same game. Now he dreaded it. It had never occurred to him that they might be facing each other as rivals.

He had hoped they would both play on the Larks -- the only team that mattered with him. But that part of his hope hadn't been realized. After all these years, the Larks had waived him out that very summer. They wanted to make way for a rookie. He had never thought the Larks' management would do a thing like that. The Champs were cold-blooded, but not the Larks. Yet he held no grudge.

Just a month later Tom had come up from the Association. In the big time he had seven wins with only one loss. Those seven wins had helped the Larks move up from third place in the late weeks of the season. The young fellow who had taken old George's place had also been a front-runner in the final lap. George came to feel it had been a wise move.

The Champs, in the other league, had picked up George in the meantime. They needed a steady pinch hitter for the stretch drive. The Champs were noted for getting the last glorious moments out of the old-timers. And George had not failed them. He knew, too, that this season was his last.

George often compared the Champs and the Larks during the closing weeks of the season as they both battled for the pennants. The Larks were like a gang of upstarts from the wrong side of the tracks. They fought up to the top and stayed there from sheer spirit and daring. He loved that spirit.

The Champs were the old imperial masters, accustomed to winning, calm, sure of themselves. They looked as confident as the Civil War generals pictured on the walls of the Old Planters Hotel where the teams used to stay.

The Champs stood poised, waiting for the other team to break. But the Larks were not breaking.

The Larks' manager had gone along with his veteran pitchers in the first three games. When he gave Tom his chance in the fourth game, the youngster had evened up the series at two and two.

George had not played in that game. But he had two pinch hits out of three times at bat in other games. He needed only one more to tie an all-time series record for singles.

Hitting was always his strength. He did not hit the long ball but punched out singles to all fields. He caught the defense off stride. It had been that way since the first Series in which he had played. Was that a full nineteen years ago, when he was just a year out of high school? It did not seem that long.

He recalled those years of high school ball, when he was known for his spirit, his steady hitting, and his ability to chase the ball out of Fairgrounds Park and catch it across the street in the neighbor's front yard. Tall and lanky, with flowing, sandy-colored hair, he seemed to float along on his long stride. But he always managed to get to the ball in time.

Most big-league scouts overlooked him. His throwing arm seemed weak. The lone scout who took a second look saw real potential -- tremendous spirit, great ballhawking, and an exceptional batting eye. George had a good first year in the minors. Three-quarters fight and one-quarter ability carried him.

The Larks' utility outfielder had been hurt late that season. Since they needed an extra outfielder for the stretch drive, they brought up George. He played mostly in the late innings when the Larks were ahead. The manager substituted him for his slow-moving left fielder. That fellow was a Ruth at bat and a rube in the field.

George remembered how he won fame early in his career back in the thirties. It was the seventh game of his first World Series, the last of the ninth. And no score!

Pepper Nelson had tripled to start the inning. But now it looked as if he would die on third. The great Lefty on the mound was showing the overflow crowd why he had won thirty games that year. It had been a momentary lapse when he threw too good a first pitch to Pepper. Now he was his old self again. He struck out Ramsey and O'Fallon, the two power hitters.

The Larks' manager called time. He walked slowly towards the spot where George leaned out of the dugout. "Can you hit this guy?" he said in a matter-of-fact way.

"I can bunt the run in," George answered confidently.

"With two outs?" The manager raised his eyebrows.

"With two outs." George responded flatly.

"Bunt the second pitch then."

Many times since then George had wondered at his brashness. A nineteen-year-old kid, facing the greatest pitcher of the decade! He could remember no fear. Only the confident sureness that he could bunt the ball and beat the throw.

Five years later he would have shaken with tension. "I was too young to know what I was doing," George explained.

"That's why I did not fear Lefty."

"Sully pinch-hitting for Hayes," the umpire announced as the overflow home crowd tensed in expectation. It was the stretch in the Kentucky Derby, set point at Wimbledon, the moment of truth before the matador drives his sword, the extra-point kick in the last second which can break a tie. It was all these - and more.

The first sizzling fast ball cut the heart of the plate. George looked at third, where Pepper danced around like a thoroughbred waiting the starting signal.

George braced his right foot as Lefty prepared to throw.

The pitch was perfect. Crack! The bunt spun out just as he had hoped.

He raced for first.

Lefty was caught off guard momentarily. Then with that pantherlike movement which made him a great fielding pitcher, he raced toward the third-base line, scooped up the ball, swung around, and fired, all in one swift, continuous motion.

George was at full stride now. He ate up yards like an antelope on his home prairie. As he touched the base with his right foot, he heard the report of the perfect throw in the first baseman's glove. The explosive roar of the crowd told him he was safe.

"Was that nineteen years ago?" George asked himself as he selected his bat carefully. It seemed to be just before this Series began. Yet in another way it appeared so long ago. The time in the middle ebbed and flowed in his memory.

The calm brashness of his first Series was gone. How could he bat against his own son? If he singled, the boy would get the blame for the loss. And if he didn't hit? For the remainder of his life, fans would say that he had thrown the game to his son.

George had always played it full tilt -- every game, every play. That's why he had lasted so much longer than players far better than he.

He looked at the little lefty on the mound. He was short and swarthy. With arms akimbo and legs apart, he stood squarely facing the plate, waiting for his father to step into the batter's box. His whole manner seemed to say: "C'mon Pop, I want to get this over with."

But George thought sadly, "It isn't going to be that easy, son. I can hit your best."

"Why can't I just strike out?" This thought flashed through his mind.

He swung his bat slowly. "I've always told Tom to give it his best. Now I've got to give everything I've got."

Still he hoped it wouldn't be necessary. He hoped something would happen. He murmured a prayer. "Maybe Tom will walk me and then strike out the next batter."

He stepped into the box.

The first pitch dispelled hopes of a walk. It cut the plate, fast and chest-high. The second was a curve which he watched sweep the outside corner.

The runner off third tried to worry young Tom. But in vain. "He'll waste one now," George thought.

But at that very moment the ball stood in front of him. It was close in, but still over. For a moment it seemed to hang in air before him. He had to swing.

George pulled hard, met the ball squarely, and sent it down the third-base line. The home-town crowd let out a roar as George raced toward first. Then a surprised "Oh" swept the stands. George sensed something was amiss. He rounded the bag and saw the left fielder fielding the ball. But the third-base umpire was giving the out signal. The runner from third was walking dejectedly from the base line toward the dugout. The ball had grazed his thigh.

The runner was out. The game was over. Little Tom had won -- but he, George, had played it straight.

He watched a crowd surge around the young hero on the mound. He smiled a very fatherly smile and recalled again the long-past day when another nineteen-year-old had won a World Series game.

"Cochems' Years"
Better the Dream

The following fall (1906), a man soon to become a legend walked onto the Saint Louis campus. Trim, dark-haired, handsome, with the stride of an athlete and the sharpness of a river-boat gambler, Eddie Cochems proved to be the most successful of the University's football coaches, and one of the nation's greatest.

Interestingly, Cochems came from a musical rather than an athletic family. He claimed direct descent from Richard Wagner on his mother's side. His twin brother, Carol, a baritone, made his operatic debut in Italy. Eddie and another brother, Henry, preferred football. While his twin brother reached for high notes at La Scala, Eddie reached the heights of American coaching.

Cochems gathered his team in Wisconsin during the last month of the summer vacation. Before returning home, Saint Louis had beaten Carroll College 22-0, Saint John's Military Academy 27-0, Lawrence College 6-0, and Marquette University 30-0. Word came down from the North of a new over-hand pass that Halfback Brad Robinson threw to Fullback Jack Schneider with amazing accuracy and distance. Local fans waited expectantly.

The team returned to Missouri and rolled over Saint Charles Military Academy 33-0, Cape Normal 59-0, Rolla 71-0, Kansas University 34-2, and the Kansas City Medics 54-0. As yet, no opponent had crossed the Blue and White goal. In one game, right half Frankie Acker scored five touchdowns, kicked nine out of nine extra points, and returned a kickoff one hundred and fifteen yards. Robinson threw a pass for an unprecedented forty-eight yards -- a record for the season.

All this, especially the Kansas University game, was too much for Professor Clark W. Hetherington, Director of the Department of Physical Education at Missouri University. When Saint Louis asked for a football game with the State University, Hetherington accused Saint Louis of using "ringers", "professionals," "transfers," and "a lot of coal-heaving huskies." Most sports writers believed Hetherington was throwing up a smoke screen because Missouri University did not have enough "coal-heaving huskies" to beat their rivals the Kansas Jayhawks. But a reporter of the Saint Louis Star decided to make a thorough investigation of the charges.

Perhaps in response to Hetherington's strictures on their lack of scholarly purpose, Cochems sent his star players, Captain Jack Kenney, Jack Schneider, Frankie Acker, and Brad Robinson to the various high schools in Saint Louis to talk on football in general, and Saint Louis University football in particular. Junior medical student Robinson wrote accounts of the football games for the school literary magazine.

The Iowa Hawkeyes came to Saint Louis for the big game of the season on Thanksgiving. Saint Louis remembered its 31-0 loss of the previous year. A sell-out crowd of twelve thousand, including much of Saint Louis' society, filled Sportsman's Park on a beautiful day to watch what a sports writer called the "most superb exhibition of football tactics ever displayed on the gridiron in our city." Saint Louis won 39-0. The Hawkeyes had one consolation. Physically they were intact. Neither side sustained an injury.

This finest team in Saint Louis University's history

95

merited public recognition as "one of the best in America and certainly the best west of the Mississippi."

By this time, the reporter for the Star had finished his thorough study of the background of the team Cochems had assembled. He found the charges unwarranted. It was true that many of the players were transfers: four from Marquette, and two from Drury College in Springfield, Missouri. Several others, including Frankie Acker, had come from Wisconsin with Eddie Cochems. But they had all been properly admitted to the Medical School of the University. And in those days a transfer student did not have to remain out of competition a year. Such an influx of players, added to a squad that had lost only once in two years, would certainly bring a good team to greatness.

The final evaluation of the college work of these men was to come later, after their gridiron days were over. Of the sixteen men who bore the brunt of the first two campaigns under Cochems, nine received their M.D. Degrees from the University, including end Captain Jack Kenney, and two sparkling backs, Edward Sarsfield Murphy, who became a skillful surgeon in Saint Louis, and Bradbury Norton Robinson, an outstanding physician in his native town of Baraboo, Wisconsin. The other football playing physicians-to-be were Joseph Brennan, Heber "Babe" De Pew, Charles Houston Orr, Louis D. Hughes, David Lamb, and Horace Archie Lowe. Frankie Acker bore the major brunt of criticism. It is true that Acker did not complete medical studies at Saint Louis University; he transferred to dentistry, practiced his profession in California, invested wisely in real estate, and amassed a most comfortable fortune.

Again the following year, Cochems' charges rolled to victories over such teams as Creighton, Kansas, Washington, and Arkansas. Games with mighty Michigan and the powerful Carlisle Indians could not be played as the respective school authorities would allow only one trip a season -- and each had gone elsewhere before their scheduled visit to Saint Louis. After the crushing victory over Nebraska, 34-0 on Thanksgiving Day before fifteen thousand spectators, Saint Louis decided to travel. This proved to be high tide.

The Blue and White played a post-season game in the Pacific Northwest. The long lay-over since Thanksgiving and the tiresome train ride took its toll. Washington State beat Saint Louis 11-0 on Christmas Day.

The football teams during Rogers' term certainly reached beyond his highest hopes. For the next forty-five years, until the University discontinued inter-collegiate football, the Blue and White fans could always assuage a losing season by looking back to the glorious days when the unforgettable four of Murphy, Acker, Robinson, and Schneider swept down the field at Grand and Dodier.

Faculty sponsor, Father Faherty, congratulates the Regis College Ski Team, winners over Idaho State and Arizona State in the Westminster Invitational at Alta, Utah. (1956)

97

Father Faherty joins with other officers of the St. Peter Canisius Writers' Guild in appraising the first copy of their publication The Catholic Writer's Magazine Market.(1945)

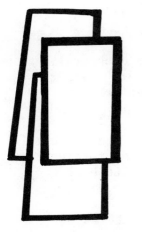

ST. LOUIS

Born and raised in St. Louis, Father Faherty has lived in Rome, Denver, in Florida, Wisconsin, and Kansas. Unlike Thoreau who was said to have travelled widely in Concord, Father Faherty has travelled widely . . . period. But throughout his travels, he has maintained a fierce loyalty to St. Louis. As a historical scholar, he knows well the value of knowing a narrowly defined subject in depth. As a writer/priest he has a vigorous and intelligent curiosity. The latter gives the former a unique kind of perspective. Just as his religion gives breadth to his writing about sports, so his travels give a rich background to his writing about St. Louis.

This section contains three shorter pieces -- excerpts from longer pieces -- and one long complete piece. Because of space limitations the reader will not find pieces like his introduction to Religious Roots of Black Catholicism in St. Louis, or parts from his history of St. Louis, or Dream by the River, or Wide River, Wide Land. Much of Barnaby Faherty's work about St. Louis centers on people who made contributions to that city. The first two selections, "I Was in Prison and You Visited Me" and "William Banks Rogers: Second Founder," show how the personality of St. Louis emerges from the strength and color of its people. Even when writing about something

99

as cold and impersonal as a grey stone cathedral, a building that overwhelms most people, Father Faherty focuses on the people involved with it. In so doing, he gives stature to the people and humanity and warmth to the cathedral.

In the final place, "Mr. Shaw's Garden," the first half produces vignettes of local and foreign people as they visit, talk about or telephone Shaw's Garden. The second half traces the history of the garden through some of its most important contributors. And through it all comes the garden itself: exploding in color, peeking through with its loveliness. A subject to contemplate, to study; a sight to enjoy. A local place to cherish and love.

"I Was in Prison and You Visited Me"
from Jesuit Bulletin, October, 1960

The phone in Father Clark's room at The Queen's Work rang late at night. Father awoke and lifted the receiver.

"Pray hard, Father," a youthful voice said. "Randy and I got a supermarket all set up. If we score on this, we're in the chips."

Experience had taught Father Clark how to deal with boys of this type. Noticing the slight uncertainty in the voice, he tried a tested technique. "This is a big job, Jim. Do I know this Randy? Is he any good? Is he jumpy with a gun? Will he fall all over himself getting out?"

"No, Father," Jim came back. "We've got it all figured out." The uncertainty was even more marked.

"Has he ever done any jobs before?" Father Clark went on. "Has he 'pushed over' a filling station? or a liquor store? Does he know any 'cons'? Does he know anybody? You'd better bring that boy down to see me."

"All right, Father." All assuredness was gone now.

At three o'clock that morning, two fellows walked into the lobby of The Queen's Work. They wore blue jeans. Their hands were in their pockets.

Father Clark greeted Jim. Then he looked at Randy, "I don't know you, son," he began. "Have you done any jobs before?"

Instead of answering, Randy turned to Jim and remarked, "Are we going to sit here all night listening to this priest 'yack?'"

"Don't talk to Father like that," Jim said, and slapped Randy in the mouth.

"Now wait a minute," Father said to Jim. "You step outside a minute. I want to talk to Randy here." Jim obeyed.

"If you want to steal, son, you ought to have someone teach you who knows how. But you don't want to steal." Then abruptly changing the tack, he asked. "Where does your mother live?"

"My father shot her," Randy answered and then began to cry.

"I'll get you a job, son. And a place to live." Father Clark clinched his advantage. Before the two boys left that evening, they had abandoned their plans for the holdup. Further, they made their first confession in months. Today they are good boys.

This is not an infrequent occurrence for Father Charles Clark. Newspapers call him "The Hoodlums' Priest." He took the second name "Dismas" in honor of the good thief, the patron of his work. He has two paintings of the Saint in his room, both the work of convicts.

"William Banks Rogers, Second Founder,"
Better the Dream

The most significant era in the history of the city of Saint Louis between the Civil War and World War II was the time of the Louisiana Purchase Exposition, the Saint Louis World's Fair. These early years of the Twentieth Century also proved to be Saint Louis University's most constructive inter-bella era. Furthermore the most influential and far-sighted administrator during this ninety year period was William Banks Rogers, University President from 1900 to 1908. By updating the "Old College," bringing it into line with American academic development, and enlarging its scope and vision, he truly rebuilt Saint Louis University.

Rogers' appearance was unimpressive. A long, thin neck stretched through a large, loose collar; above an oversized forehead, black hair sat like a dark skull-cap on the back of his head. His eyes stared intently out of wire-framed glasses. Small, frail, forty-three year old Rogers looked more like a clerk than a college president. Physically he would have made an excellent Bob Cratchet for a stage version of Dickens' Christmas Carol.

Rogers did not seem the man to battle the unconcern for public image that gripped so many of his confreres; the over-concentration on the classical tradition; and the power and independent purposes of the scholasticate establishment.

Rogers was a tirelessly energetic little man, brilliant of mind, eminently practical, and ready to try his own fine ideas and those of others. His business-like manner in ordinary dealings with faculty and students made him admired long before he was liked. With the alumni, however, this admiration rapidly changed into deep affection.

Immediately upon finishing his course of studies, he became dean of students, then chancellor and a member of the Board of Trustees of Saint Louis University. He served two years as President of Marquette in Milwaukee; then returned to Saint Louis in 1900.

Not by nature a gregarious or out-going man, he realized that he had to move widely among the leaders of the civic community to build the university he envisioned. Traditionally, the President of Saint Louis University had no office or secretary. Rogers carried on an amazing correspondence by hand in his own room. Sometimes he would work until four in the morning, or fall asleep at his desk several hours after midnight.

Another man might have set up an office and hired a secretary. Unwisely, Rogers did not do so. Parsimonious by temperament, he abstained from comforts and conveniences, even when his work suggested such. While he was engaged in large public ventures for the University, he overlooked many needed domestic improvements. While personally frugal, he was most generous toward needy students, even personally arranging low-cost lodging for them.

When Rogers came to Saint Louis University, the institution had been buried behind walls in downtown Saint Louis for so long that the mere arrival on the Grand campus a decade before could not move it back in to the center of community life. Rogers broke down the walls. He placed Saint Louis University in the heart of civic and academic affairs. He gained the support and advice of a group of outstanding business executives. He participated intimately in Saint Louis' great concern of the time -- the World's Fair. He built a sound athletic program.

Educationally, Rogers moved the University ahead so rapidly that in less than a decade it had surged back into the American academic mainstream.

Rogers was intent on making Saint Louis University a

recognized American university. He wanted to bring about cooperation and mutual help among the Catholic and secular schools of the city, state, and nation. He was desirous of developing the good will of the clergy and people of Saint Louis.

Within the Jesuit faculty, he wished to develop a distinctly American outlook in the field of secondary and higher education. The trends of his administration, and his words at such meetings as the National Catholic Educational Association, showed this high goal. He tried the unbelievably difficult task of making a Jesuit Province . . . acutely aware of the need of public relations and zealous for the academic apostolate.

To secure these goals, he built up a strong supporting team of men who understood and appreciated his purposes. In turn, he was ready to accept and recognize their good ideas. He gave them tasks to do and confident support in those tasks.

By persuasion, rather than administrative ukase he urged his fellow Jesuits to reassess their classic-centered curriculum and particularized approach to philosophy in the light of American realities. He began the University's initial scholarly publication by inviting faculty members to publish in the reorganized official Bulletin of the school. He joined the Missouri Union of Colleges. He offered the University facilities for the first annual meeting of the Catholic Educational Association. He set up the high school as a distinct unit and lengthened the college course to four years. He won a place for science in a literary-oriented institution. He brought the Marion Sims-Beaumont Medical School into the orbit of the University; and thus, once again, the "old college" gained true university status. He prepared for the affiliation of a law school. He welcomed President Theodore Roosevelt to the campus, the first President of the United States to visit the school while in office.

These tremendous achievements seemed beyond the capacity of a physically small, unspectacular, and retiring man. Cursory observers overlooked Rogers' burning enthusiasm, his dogged self-sacrificing performance of the smallest task, and his universality in dealing with people. Father Laurence Kenny, who knew him well, made this judgment many years later: "Perhaps the art of Father Rogers lay in the fact that he could meet any character of person, from the little child in the street to the President of the United States with perfectly natural ease and direct the conversation.

103

How he acquired this power is a mystery; he was never voluble; he was in no wise naturally favored in form or feature, but his mind was fertile in ideas of practical good things that others as well as he himself could accomplish. Thus he was enabled to secure the fullest cooperation not only of every member of his community . . . but also the good will of the most diverse characters of the local citizenry."

A tribute to Rogers has remained undimmed for over fifty years. A writer in 1911 placed his name "with those of . . . the founders of the University." He rightly deserves the title "Second Founder of Saint Louis University."

"St. Louis' Great 'New' Cathedral"
from Missouri Life, 1974

Archbishop Joseph Elmer Ritter arrived at Union Station the following October while most of the city listened to the play-by-play of the World Series between the Cardinals and the Red Sox. The new Archbishop had none of Glennon's grandeur of manner, impressive presence, or oratorical skill. His qualities were less conspicuous but equally significant. He reminded many over the years of another "man from Missouri" who also happened to be right on the big issues so many times, President Harry S. Truman.

Ritter expressed his views on architecture: "No matter how much we may prefer Gothic or Byzantine and Roman architecture, it would be wrong and unnatural to think that artists of our day . . . must constantly go back to the past in art and architecture." As a result of this conviction, he gave free rein to pastors and architects who wanted to try the new. Such churches as St. Peter's in Kirkwood, St. Ann's in Normandy, and Resurrection in St. Louis attest this attitude.

His openness to the new, however, did not cause him to disdain tradition. He heeded the advice of experts. As a result, he wanted advances at the cathedral consistent with the style and original planning: a new sacristy on the north end of the building, extensive mechanical improvements, and an expansion of mosaic art. Seventy-five per cent of all the mosaics in the cathedral went in during Cardinal Ritter's twenty-one years.

He found the creation of a mosaic so fascinating that

often during his two decades in Missouri he went to the Heuduck studio unannounced to watch Paul and Arno at their work and listen to their description of the specific section they worked on at the time.

* * *

Before entering, a visitor should take a careful look at the whole impressive Romanesque exterior. He will see a facade with twin towers, a rose window over the center door, and a green-tiled dome in the shape of an inverted goblet. Even a look at the hand-carved doors rewards the viewer. Thousands of people pass through them without realizing what an impressive work of art they are.

Most vestibules are simply places for a moment's pause before entering a church; but the vestibule of the great cathedral contains some of the finest mosaics in the whole world. Ten panels depict events of the life of the crusading king, St. Louis IX of France, who gave his name to the city and the archdiocese.

Upon entering the Cathedral, the visitor does not appreciate immediately the full immensity of the building-- a common experience in a Byzantine interior. As a result, he should walk up the middle aisle at once to the widest part of the structure. The size of the edifice will awe him. The distance from the front door to the north wall is 238 feet. The width across the transepts is 195 feet. The central dome soars above him to a height of 143 feet. Half of the churches of the country could fit under it.

The main altar follows tradition and blends with the pattern of the church. The elaborate statuary on the altar presents the crucified Christ with his Mother Mary and Apostle John looking up at him. Over the altar a baldachin, or canopy, rises, a smaller replica of the external dome of the Cathedral, supported by fourteen colums of various Italian marbles. Statues of Matthew, Mark, Luke and John look down from the side of the baldachin.

* * *

At this point the visitor can look directly above him where the red and gold central dome sparkles with the brilliance of a sunset. As a model for the face of God in the mosaic, the Polish-born artist John de Rosen chose the Orthodox Patriarch Athenagoras, who, many believe, is physically the most impressive clergyman of our times. Perhaps John de Rosen, because of his Polish heritage, looked on Siberia as the "hell" of his universe. In the south arch beneath this central dome, the Arch of Judgment, the people on Christ's left who are turning their backs on his saving message walk not toward the fires of Hell but, instead, into the snow and cold of unrequited love.

* * *

Our generation does not express its devotion to God in outbursts of enthusiasm for erecting temples of worship. In fact, we do build beautiful churches and synagogues, and occasionally, a costly cathedral. But we do this quietly, to mute complaints that modern man could better spend his money for hospitals and clinics or in providing social services for the poor. The generation of youthful Archbishop Glennon--rich and poor--built hospitals, orphanages, schools, seminaries and churches--as well as the Cathedral.

The building cost between seven and eight million dollars. Those who criticize such an outlay should recall that this figure is far less than half what an aircraft carrier cost at that time. The mosaics in the cathedral will still inspire their great-great-grandchildren in the year 2075, long after the carrier has rusted into nothingness. The critic should contrast the green-tiled dome on Lindell with the superdome in New Orleans--one a temple for the worship of God, the other a monument to a monstrous ambition to out-hustle Houston.

So on your next visit to Saint Louis, see the Arch and the Old Cathedral on the waterfront, Shaw's Garden, Busch Stadium, McDonnell Planetarium, Grant's Farm or the zoo. But save a few hours for the Great Cathedral.

If you can, enter the Cathedral late in the day. Then, the late afternoon sun plays, at once, gloriously and subtly on the gleaming mosaics. Every turn of your head brings new panoramas of beauty. And the silence of the waning day, with the warmth of the sun, may instill the thought that God views kindly this monument to Him built by man.

"Mr. Shaw's Garden"
from <u>Missouri Life</u>, 1976

On his first European trip, a resident of Missouri took a bus tour around the city of London. He became intrigued with the guide's constant references to the Royal Garden at Kew as the second most important botanical garden in the world. Finally, he asked: "Where is the most important garden?"

"In a place in the States called St. Louis," the Englishman responded. "The Missouri Botanical Garden, locally known as Shaw's Garden."

Laughing at himself, the Missourian said to his fellow

106

sightseers: "I came three thousand miles to see the second most important gardens, and I haven't even visited Shaw's Garden, six blocks from my home."

Fortunately, every year fewer and fewer Missourians have to admit their failure to visit what may not necessarily reach the English tour guide's high estimate, but which certainly ranks among the finest gardens in the entire world and the most vital in the United States. Further, while taxes support the Kew Garden in England, the Berlin Garden in Germany, and the New York Botanical Garden, the Missouri Botanical Garden has never received financial support from the taxpayers of the city or the state. To the amazement of all who hear about it, the Garden actually paid a large tax assessment until recent times, and even today pays for water, gas, electricity and every other charge the state and city levy against private enterprise.

Taxpayers finance the fish diet of the sea elephant at the St. Louis Zoo, but the legacy of an English-born St. Louis businessman, Henry Shaw, other private contributions, and the support of such organizations at "The Members of the Garden," have nourished Shaw's orchids and chrysanthemums to their glorious growth.

Had the Missourian mentioned above walked the six blocks from his home to the Garden at any season of the year, he could have seen plants from all parts of the world on display in their natural settings. In the spring, over sixty-five thousand bulbs flame with vibrant color amid the blossoming trees and the green promise of nature aborning In mid-summer more than twenty species of water lilies bloom in reflecting pools. Roses on top of roses, thousands of blooms, in four terraces, blaze in every fragrant hue. At other seasons of the year, the visitor might gaze in awe at the display of chrysanthemums, orchids, or Christmas flowers.

Within the Graden walls, he would find an ever-changing, always lovely natural progression. He could come every week, and never find a sight exactly like the previous one, an experience he could match only if he lived near high mountains and witnessed the ever-changing panorama of cloud formations on the peak. He would also learn that he had come to a research and educational center dedicated to the study of botany and horticulture, not merely a place of endless beauty but a seed-bed of learning and a source of community enrichment.

The visitor sees a surprising variety of buildings. As he enters the main gate, the Climatron immediately ahead of

him would first grab his attention. So impressive is it,
that he might fail to notice the Garden Gate shop, with its
wide selection of botanically related gifts, and books on
gardening, botany and natural history. He will probably
browse in this area after he has toured the entire Garden.
He may hardly be aware, even, of the lily ponds between the
entrance and the geodesic dome.

At night the Climatron looks like the moon just peeking
over the horizon. Hardly less impressive during the full
flood of the noon-day sun, the building boasts over two
thousand distinct species of plants, systematically selected
from the tropical regions of the world. By maintaing dif-
ferences in climate in the building, botanists simulate the
varied environments of those areas. The collection demon-
strates important truths about plants and about the plant
world's relationship to man. Men and plants should be
partners. Plants can get along without men, but man can't
survive without them. Project Apollo, the short stay of a
few astronauts on the lifeless surface of the moon, made men
aware in a dramatic way of the life-giving qualities of
man's home, planet earth.

One frequent Garden visitor said, "While the Climatron
always fascinates me, I especially like to come here on a
drab November day. Outside everything is gray and raw;
inside brightness and warmth!"

To the south of the Climatron, the Desert House offers
a view of cacti and other juice-rich plants found only in
the dry regions of the world. The man-made arid environment
brings to mind the prospector heading for the distant mountains in search of gold, or the shepherd seeking a pool of
water for his sheep on the way to the grass of the higher
hills. The glass-encased, semi-cylindrical building with
end walls to the front and rear resembles a Quonset hut of
World War II in shape, except that it is a bit taller and
narrower.

Matching the Desert House in form, the sixty-year old
building immediately north of the Climatron recently changed
its character. Formerly it housed the Garden's collection
of juicy plants--"succulents" is the scientific term--of the
Old World. To open the Bicentennial Year, this building
became the first greenhouse in the nation devoted exclusively to the display of plants from the five Mediterranean
climatic regions of the world, characterized by cool, moist
winters and hot, dry summers. These areas are the Mediterranean Sea basin, southern California, central Chile, the
Cape Province of South Africa and southern Australia.

Young, energetic Dr. Peter H. Raven, Garden director and originator of the project, stated that the building would contain more than 250 different plant species, some extremely rare and in danger of extinction. Others, such as the grape, olive and fig, form part of the staple economy of those areas.

The involvement of "Hill 2000," an organization of the Italian-American neighborhood immediately west of the Garden, in the dediction of the Mediterranean House, highlighted a new trend in the development of the Garden. St. Louis has enclaves of various Mediterranean nationalities, besides the Italians of the "Hill": a colony of Catalans from the northeast coast of Spain, numerous citizens of Greek extraction, a well-knit group of Lebanese, and many people of Jewish background, few of whom, however, actually came to America from the area of modern Israel. In his dedicatory address, Dr. Raven addressed the Mediterranean House as a symbol of the resurgence of the entire St. Louis area and of the value of preserving old neighborhoods, such as the one immediately east of the Garden.

The next building to the north, the Floral Display House, exhibits major flower shows and special displays by horticultural societies. In the greenhouse setting of the plant shop adjoining it, the visitor can browse, and if he or she wishes, select plants at moderate prices. In that area, too, one can interrupt the visit with lunch or refreshments.

Beyond this area, in the northwestern corner of the Garden lie growing, propagating and servicing areas. In the northeast section, the visitor walks through the perennial garden and the old rose park to the oldest greenhouse in continuous operation west of the Mississippi, the Linnaean House, built by Henry Shaw himself. It houses the Garden's famous collection of camellias.

The path beside the east wall leads past the main entrance to the southeast corner of the Garden. Here stand the administration building, the director's residence, the restored Tower Grove House, the home of the man most responsible for the Garden, Henry Shaw, who gave his name and much of his fortune to the institution, and the John S. Lehmann Building. This glass-walled structure houses the herbarium, a library containing over seventy-five thousand volumes on horticultural and botanical subjects, and the Department of Education.

West of the Lehmann Building, the visitors walks through the English Woodland Garden, where six hundred

azaleas and dozens of new attractive plants will catch his
eye -- thanks in part to the generosity of the Ladue Garden
Club. The participation of this St. Louis County garden
club points to another feature: the Garden's cooperation
with societies similarly dedicated, such as the National
Council of State Garden Clubs, and the voluntary participation of many Missouri citizens in a variety of projects. In
1975 alone, volunteers contributed a total of thirty-five
thousand work hours.

The next stop on the tour of the Garden sends the visitor half-way around the world from Sherwood Forest to the
foot of Mt. Fujiyama. To many Americans, the term "Japanese
Garden" brings to mind the lovely setting in the opera
"Madame Butterfly" where Cio-Cio-San and Lieutenant Pinker-
ton sang their love duet at the end of the first act. To
the Japanese themselves, a traditional garden expresses
certain characteristics they deem unique to their people,
closeness to nature, a tendency to suggest rather than
describe explicitly, a preference for asymmetry of design
and a concern for simplicity. Even if they build their
homes in a non-Japanese style, they will retain the traditional garden.

The Japanese American Citizens League of Greater St.
Louis promoted the initial steps in the development of the
first Japanese Garden in the central part of the United
States. A leading Japanese landscape architect, Koichi
Kawana, was responsible for the overall design.

The directors of the Missouri Botanical Garden chose
the southwestern section of the property, hitherto not
usually open to the public. Its main feature, a lake, will
form a central focus for bridges, a teahouse, a tiny water-
fall, lanterns, and small gardens of varying style displayed
against beautifully landscaped background. Dr. Raven set
the date for the opening of the Japanese Garden during the
Bicentennial year.

And Dr. Raven has other plans, such as a Home Landscaping Demonstration Center for the area west of the Climatron. Demonstration gardens will encircle a model home unit
that will contain a small classroom, a library on domestic
landscaping, storage and work areas and a greenhouse. Each
demonstration garden will have a flavor of its own, empha-
sizing indoor-outdoor living, to show by example the proper
relationships of home and surroundings.

The seventy-nine acre Garden stretches eight blocks
along the west side of Tower Grove Avenue between Shaw
Avenue on the north and Magnolia on the south, in the cen-

110

tral-southwest section of St. Louis. Alfred Avenue, the
west limit of the Garden, turns a little east of straight
north as it approaches Shaw Avenue, so that the area does
not form a perfect rectangle.

Interstate Highway 44 passes two blocks north of the
Garden, with east and west exits not far away, so that the
out-of-town visitor can readily reach the Garden area. He
had better have a good back-seat driver to keep an eye on
the carefully marked but tricky turns to the Garden itself
once he leaves the Interstate. St. Louis area visitors can
easily reach the Garden on such thoroughfares as Kingshighway, Grand, Vandeventer, and Arsenal that pass in the
vicinity. They can park within the Garden Wall, turning in
from Tower Grove Avenue just south of Shaw Avenue, a few
yards north of the Main Entrance.

In 1974, three hundred thousand guests visited the
Garden, a seven per cent increase over the previous year.
Missourians naturally led in numbers, with Illinoisans not
far behind, a surprising number of them from the Chicago
area. The Midwest sends most visitors, and the South and
Southwest their share. Among foreign countries, West German
has more than its share, usually tourists visiting relatives
in Missouri.

Foreign students enjoy the Garden too, principally
medical students from India, Japan, Pakistan, who reside in
the area east of the Garden not too far from the St. Louis
University Medical Complex. A husband and wife team of students came from Saudi Arabia. Another interesting visitor
was an Alaskan Eskimo who served at the time in the Air
Force at Scott Field.

Questioning of the visitors or overhearing of their
remarks as they walk through the Garden points out the
particular interests that prompted them to come. The
flowers, the plants and the Climatron seem to be the favorite attractions.

While the casual visitor may merely feel the awe of the
beauty of the Garden, more serious observers will realize
that it contribute significantly to human survival. Research and analysis combine in this important task. This
means collecting, and classifying all plants.

Garden scientists journey throughout the world in quest
of knowledge to help man understanding his environment. The
herbarium contains almost two and a half million specimens,
and can accommodate more than a million others. This vast
assortment includes the best collection of African plants in
the western hemisphere, the world's best collection of

Panamanian plants, and steadily more complete collections from Europe, Africa, and the Americas.

In cooperation with the Smithsonian Tropical Research Institute, the Garden maintains a tropical field station in the Canal Zone. It exchanges information and specimens with other institutions.

Of special interest to Missourians, it serves as a center for identifying Missouri's endangered flora. Thus it helps save irreplaceable species from being forever lost. It introduces new flowers and plants, hitherto not common to the area. Two decades ago, for instance, most Missourians knew azaleas--if they had ever heard of them--only from friends who had visited Mobile or Natchez or from songs of the Deep South. Since then, botanists at the Garden have encouraged their local growth.

Such a wide-ranging program requires a first-rate staff, with experts in a variety of fields from the classification of plants and their geographical distribution to the study of development of genes and cells. The Missouri Botanical Garden has just such a staff. As an indication of their skill, in the first half of the Seventies, they wrote more than two hundred scientific papers, a feat that would make most university faculties proud.

Mention of universities points to another facet of the Garden's wide area of public service. A regional center of higher learning, the Garden works closely with the universities of the metropolitan area. Many professional scientists in a variety of related fields come to the Garden for advanced study. The Garden publishes the Missouri Botanical Garden Bulletin and a scientific quarterly called the Annals of the Missouri Botanical Garden.

To reach the amateur botanist and gardener, the Garden distributes booklets of a highly practical nature. In these days of high food costs, one of these, Inflation Gardening, has caught the attention of many. The staff organizes field trips to botanically interesting areas, sponsors a Summer Nature Study Program, provides courses for adults, and conducts classes and workshops during the school year that forty thousand school children attended as part of their classroom instruction. In 1976, for instance, thirty-five hundred people came to the spring garden workshop.

Every April, the Garden sponsors a plant clinic, when amateur gardeners may bring their diseased plants for consultation or otherwise discuss plant problems. It sponsors a plant sale, usually in October, when the supply of plant material on hand and the demands of those interested in gardening coincide. It features a Horticultural Show in May and a Cactus show in late July or early August. The fall schedule keeps the Head of its Education Department, Mr. Ken Peck, constantly finishing one program and preparing for another.

The Garden, too, serves as an information center both for the expert researcher as well as the amateur who needs to verify a point of information or hearsay. A local author, for instance, called one day to check a statement he intended to use in a western story.

The receptionist read his words over the loud speaker in the Desert House, pronouncing each syllable with the utmost care: "A local writer wishes to say: 'Like the cactus plant that sends its root down deep into the soil.' Is that correct?"

A male voice answered, with a touch of disgust in his tone: "Botanically, yes. Grammatically, tell him to get rid of the 'down.'"

Countless men and women have helped make Shaw's Garden what it is. In doing this, they have surpassed the vision of an English-born Saint Louis merchant, Henry Shaw, who made a relatively large fortune in the 1820's and 1830's.

In 1840 he purchased a tract of prairie land about a mile and a half square, west of Grand between Arsenal Street and Lafayette Avenue, that stretched to the King's Highway, and included a race track and a grove of trees. In that year, while checking his ledgers, he noticed that he had made a profit of $25,000--a sum he considered more than any man in his circumstances ought to make in a single year. As a result he decided to retire from business. The next year he did so, with a fortune of a quarter of a million dollars. This amazing fact makes Shaw stand out among his fellow Anglo-American businessmen who were coming to rate acquisitiveness among the finest of human qualities. He simply discontinued his money-making efforts and turned his attention to other things.

Up to that time, he had taken no part in civic affairs, had shown no interest in politics and had worked for no public charities. He had participated only slightly in the social life of St. Louis, to the dismay of many a prospective mother-in-law who eyed Shaw's growing bank account, and knew his reputation as a gentle tempered man, friendly in social relationships though shrewd and demanding in business dealings. A friend has left the opinion that Shaw had intended to return to his native land and marry an English girl, and for that reason avoided social activities in St.

Louis. His main recreation seems to have been horseback riding.

His first impulse on retiring was to travel and further his education. He spent much of the early Forties overseas, with occasional trips back to St. Louis. During 1849 in the grove of oaks on his extensive property he built a house with a central tower that gave the name Tower Grove to the area.

In early 1851, Shaw sailed back to London for the first World's Fair. He visited the Horticultural Display at the Crystal Palace and carried a letter of introduction to Sir William Hooker, the director of the world-famous botanical garden at Kew. Historians have as yet discovered no evidence that he did in fact visit the Kew Garden.

After his London trip, he returned to St. Louis and began to study books on botany. He expressed his first definite interest in beginning a botanical garden in 1853. By 1855 he had finished preliminary plans. James Reed, currently head librarian at the garden Shaw was to found, states that some observers trace Shaw's interest in botany back to his schools days in England. He had attended the Mill Hill School on the estate of Peter Collinson, a distinguished botanist. Be that as it may, in 1856 Shaw sought the advice of botanist Dr. George Engelman, who had recently founded the Academy of Science in St. Louis.

When Engelman could not convince Shaw to set up a botanical library and museum in the Garden, Engelman enlisted the aid of Sir William Hooker, director of the Kew Garden. Sir William's histrionics succeed where Dr. George's scientific approach had failed. Engelman deplored the fact that "soft soaping"--as the Western phrase is--had more effect on Shaw than sound argument. Later Engelman enlisted the aid of the Harvard botanist Asa Gray, "Mr. American Botany" from 1830 to 1890.

Even though Engelman felt that Shaw did not possess adequate scientific knowledge or taste and acted "as tough as any Scotchman," Shaw had boundless energy and a business-like way of handling matters. By 1858 he had erected the gateway, built a plant house and a rosarium, and planned a museum, a library and herbarium. He modeled these last three after the Kew pattern and completed them within two years. At the advice of Engelman and Asa Gray, he hired botanist August Findler as curator of the herbarium.

In shortly over ten years, the Garden became a major attraction for those visiting St. Louis. The early list of visitors included Horace Greeley, Asa Gray and Sir Joseph

Hooker, director of the Kew Garden, son of the earlier director with whom Shaw had corresponded. In his book, Life on the Mississippi, Mark Twain wrote approvingly of Forest Park, then went on to say: "There are other parks, and fine ones, notably Tower Grove and the Botanical Gardens; for St. Louis interested herself in such improvements at an earlier day than most of our cities."

Twain's remark brings into focus another project of Henry Shaw. He had long wanted to give to the city the property bounded by Grand, Arsenal, Kingshighway and Magnolia, just south of the Garden, for use as a park. At the time it lay just west of the city limits that ran along Grand Avenue. This proposal required action of the State Legislature as well as the city government. The hard-bargaining businessman presented the property in such a manner that the city had to take care of the park, and he became comptroller. In this way, he directed city money in developing a personal dream in the interests of the citizens of Missouri.

In his original plan, he wanted residences to border the area, both to provide living conditions in a park-like atmosphere, and to secure revenues to keep up the park. His plans also seemed to call for planned courts and non-through streets in the adjacent area to supplant the unimaginative square blocks of the rest of the city. Several of these developed during his lifetime; and one, Gurney Court, just west of the Garden, after his death. He wanted the entire Tower Grove neighborhood to be a unique district full of trees and flowers. The park itself became a paradise of pergolas, pagodas, statues of artists and explorers, and a variety of trees, native and imported, equalled by few parks in the nation.

Shaw's English background showed in the development of the park. While continental Europeans tended to over-plan with intricately shaped flower beds and the unnatural trimming of trees, the English tradition did not tend to dominate or reform nature, but to work with it, to provide open vistas, and allow trees to develop in their natural state, with a minimum of judicious trimming to aid growth.

The dedication of the Linnaean Greenhouse in 1882 marked the completion of the Garden as Shaw envisioned it. He had one last proposal, external to the Garden, at a meeting of the board of directors on June 8, 1885: the setting up of a school of botany as a special department of Washington University that would bear his name; the establishment of a professorship of botany, called after Dr. Geo-

115

rge Engleman who had died in the meantime; and the invitation of Professor William Trelease of the University of Wisconsin to hold that chair. Shaw did not live to see this proposal fulfilled in its entirely. He died on August 25, 1889.

The following month, immediately after the probating of Shaw's will, the Trustees of the Garden elected Professor Trelease as first director. Trelease gave wise guidance immediately. First, he made necessary physical repairs. Then he began a series of annual reports that helped to make the Garden more widely known.

As an early result of the Trelease efforts, Dr. E. Lewis Sturtevant of Massachusetts gave his extensive collection of medieval and modern botanical works, a major step in ranking the library among the finest in the world. Trelease commissioned the publication of a small handbook describing the Garden. He awarded the Henry Shaw medal to outstanding amateur gardeners; built the huge lily ponds, and commissioned a master plan for the future development of the Garden. He was to remain director until 1912.

Between World War I and World War II, one man and one new addition influenced the development of Shaw's germinal ideas. Edgar Anderson, a botanical genius in the field of genetics, directed the Garden for only a brief period, but he remained a dominant influence from 1930 to 1969. Concerned with scientific research and educational activities, he kept the name of the Garden known to botanists and spread its fame among ordinary citizens. His personal scientific contributions included the introduction of Bulgarian Ivy into the United States.

In the early Twenties, air pollution killed large numbers of plants at the Garden. The director purchased 1650 acres, near Gray's Summit, thirty-five miles southwest of St. Louis, for an alternate development, called the arboretum. The development of the arboretum over the years since its founding is a story in its own right, too extensive to relate here.

For many years, Shaw's estate entirely supported the Garden. Since the mid-Twentieth Century, however, the Garden has had to rely on other forms of assistance, with its endowment reaching slightly less than a fourth of its support.

Missourians have a debt to pay to one of their great pioneers, Henry Shaw. They can pay that debt in many ways. The simplest -- they can visit the Garden and bring friends. They can come again, and again, especially when they have guests from other states. They can become "Members of the Garden," by paying a tax-deductible fee, and enjoy many special events and visitation privileges, use the reference library, and receive all Garden publications.

They should talk about the Garden to their family, their neighbors, their friends. They should brag about it to their out-of-state associates, so that when visitors come to Missouri for whatever purpose, a convention, a visit, or simply a drive-through on the way elsewhere, they too will stop and see Henry Shaw's legacy, the Missouri Botanical Garden. They'll save themselves a trip to England -- or anywhere else -- to see one of the finest gardens in the world.

Here stands a priest comfortable in his flock: Father Faherty surrounded by students and fellow faculty at a Saint Louis University sporting event.

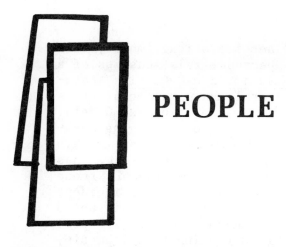

PEOPLE

A reader of Father Faherty finds history not of events but of people, people creating and responding to events. Those who know him as a priest know a man who sees God's work as work with people. Those who know him through his fiction and spiritual writings discover a man intensely interested in people. Even Father Faherty's casual conversations are peppered with references to students he taught twenty-five years ago in Denver, friends from Epiphany Parish in St. Louis where he grew up, or someone he met a week earlier playing tennis. These people are always described, not just in terms of their accomplishments, but with his constant attention to and interest in their relationships with others. He judges historical figures and contemporaries alike: not just by what changes they have made in the world, but by their personal interactions. And he loves the underdog best. This section shows his interest in people in a range of writings from sermon and eulogy to fiction and history.

In the first selection, the text of Father Faherty's eulogy for Father Claude Heithaus, S.J., there is not vague praise for a friend and colleague but a warm cataloguing of that man's accomplishments and his impact on people. The excerpt from the Lucy Stone biographical sketch, while never losing sight of her historical import, is a lively picture of the personal relationships of a public figure. In A Wall for San Sebastian, Father Faherty created several endearing characters such as the husband and wife, Cayetano and Gisela. In this excerpt, we see Don Julio, the aging Spanish land-owner who has little awareness of his real circumstances but whose personality has earned him the loyalty and affection of those close to him. Father Faherty uses an incident from the life of Pope John XXIII as a springboard for a sermon in which he described what is, perhaps, the basis for this attention to all people, significant and insignificant, leaders and followers, winners and losers: that Christ's message includes the importance of human warmth and "loving approachability." In no place is this clearer than in Faherty's Chaucerian acceptance of the faults of the bigot in his story "Doug X." As a priest, Father Faherty gets closer to people than most non-priests can and clearly accepts Christ's admonition to hate the sin and love the sinners.

The last selection, "French Nun with an American Dream," an article on the life of Phillipine Duchesne, offers a typical Faherty combination, solid historical data enlivened by a real sense of the personality of his subject and his own affection for and appreciation of her accomplishments.

"Father Claude H. Heithaus, S.J."
The Jesuit Bulletin, September, 1976

Father Claude Heithaus went to God at an opportune time. Had he been able to choose the time himself, he could have found no other more fitting moment. French Consul General Philippe Olivier had honored him just days before; his colleagues in the Historical Association of Greater St. Louis elected him president that same evening; and the Jesuit Community of Saint Louis University toasted his achievements the night before he died. He had gathered together an amazing collection of historic treasures of the Missouri Province and earlier Jesuits who worked in the Midwest, and he had organized the museum to contain them and arranged for its permanence. He went to his Maker with a clear conscience; he had closed the book.

Many will recall that Claude Heithaus once put his position at St. Louis University on the line for what he believed he had to do. He gave a remarkable address in the College Church on February 11, 1944, acclaimed throughout the country in favor of what proved the most historic step the University took in the Twentieth Century, namely leading the way among universities of former slave states in breaking the race barrier eleven years before the Warren Decision. Letters of praise poured in from all parts of the United States. The priest-chairman of the Archdiocesan Clergy Conference on Negro Welfare wrote of the speech's "profound effect for good." Black students entered St. Louis University that summer.

Father Heithaus is also well remembered for his recent work in setting up, with the assistance of Fr. Robert Doyle, S.J., John Flerlage and others, the St. Stanislaus Museum at Florissant, Missouri, and his collecting a treasure of materials that deal with the past history of the Jesuits in the Midwest. Basic to his work lay the conviction that only if we root our present efforts in the traditions and spirit handed down to us by the heroes of the past can we hope to live creative lives in the future.

During his graduate studies Fr. Heithaus spent many years looking over the relics of ancient Greek and Roman civilizations, destroyed by various waves of barbarians over the centuries. He carried his love for the past into a world where modern barbarians were using the headache ball on many historic buildings. He suddenly found that his ancient interest was a modern "in" thing, as countless Americans became concerned about their past.

He saw the St. Stanislaus Seminary Rock Building as the focal point of one of the most amazing developments in the entire history of the Church in the United States, and he set out to save it. He pointed out that the building had been at the heart of a remarkable missionary effort among the Indians of the Northwest, missions associated with the names of Fathers DeSmet, Point, Hoecken, Kuppens and others. Only two other monuments of the Catholic Church in the Midwest rivaled it -- the old Cathedrals of St. Louis and Bardstown, Kentucky. Architectural beauty combines with historic significance to make the Rock Building at Florissant a fitting place to house the Jesuit memorabilia that he so painstakingly gathered over the years.

Thus he left to his students, his friends, his city,

A PRIEST FOR ALL REASON

the St. Louis Jesuit Community, the Missouri Province, and
the Church of the Midwest a rich legacy. We are sorry to
see him go; nonetheless we can recognize a compeleted task,
a sense of conviction, a willingness to stand up for the
right as God gave him to see the right - and we pray that
God will give us the same sense of devotion.

from "Lucy Stone"
previously unpublished

One of her listeners who became interested in woman's
rights in general, and in one advocate of woman's rights in
particular, was able, charming Henry Blackwell. His pro-
gresssive and prominent family included the first American
woman to receive a diploma in medicine.

Henry had no easy task in convincing Lucy that marriage
would not hinder the work to which she had devoted her life.
Promising to collaborate for the cause of woman's rights, he
convinced her that they could accomplish more as a team than
as individuals.

They shared a dislike of the Blackstonian interpreta-
tion of the wife's legal position in marriage, and together
drew up a protest against it. As a public indication of
their protest, Lucy, with Henry's consent, did not use his
name, Blackwell, but prefixed the title Mrs. to her own
maiden name, Stone. This flaunting of custom caused no end
of comment, confusion, and lifting of eyebrows, especially
on the part of hotel clerks.

When their only daughter, Alice, came to write a biography of her mother many years later, she testified that
the union was a happy one, that her mother was a good house-
keeper and an excellent parent, and that she, Alice, suffered no neglect even while her parents were on lecture
tours.

As Henry Blackwell had predicted, Lucy and he were able
to work more effectively together. His business ability and
practical resourcefulness reinforced her idealism and zeal.
Beginning in Kansas in 1867, the Blackwells gave an ever-
present sense of balance to the suffrage struggle during the
long decades of campaigning.

from A Wall for San Sebastian

The priest rode along the dry stream, and through the

122

gap. Beyond lay a wide pleasant valley. Half-way up the hillside to the north stood a low white house, its wide arms reaching out to greet him as he approached.

As he admired the house, he caught sight of a rider coming out to meet him.

"Welcome to Vega Verde, mi padre," the mounted man said warmly as he approached. "I am Julio Mena."

"Thank you, Don Julio," he responded. "I am Fray Leon, the new missioner at San Sebastian."

He wondered momentarily why no one had even mentioned Don Julio's name. But then he had been at San Sebastian such a short time. And few villagers had said much to him about anything.

For the first time since his arrival, the picture seemed a little brighter. In this part of his parish, at least, hope still walked its uplifting way. He looked up at the older man.

Mounted on his skittish sorrel, Don Julio was a noble figure. All grayness and grandeur, he wore an inconquerable dignity even though obviously in the twilight of his years.

"Shortly after the village of San Sebastian was laid out," he began expansively, "the King gave to my grandfather all this valley of the Tarascan -- as we call this rivu-let -- the meadowland on both sides down its junction with the Conchos, and endless square miles of grazing lands in the hills behind us."

Padre Leon looked in admiration at the entire estab-lishment. "Could I ask ---?" he began.

But Don Julio pushed right on. "You are seeing the center of the finest hacienda in the valley of the Conchos. Our subsidiary ranches cover the territory for miles around. Our cattle number into thousands." Don Julio gestured gran-dly. "Do stay for dinner," he invited.

"You are kind, Don Julio," Padre Leon answered. "I will be most happy to stay."

When Don Julio dismounted, the grandeur of his appear-ance vanished. He was surprisingly short. His shoulders were not broad and one was narrower than the other. His oversized nose had given strength to his face when seen from below. But as Padre Leon looked down on it, the nose simply seemed too much for the rest of his visage.

They walked into a cool patio and sat down. The ser-vant brought each a glass of delicious wine.

"May I ask you," Padre Leon broke the silence, "about our Comanche friends to the north of th river?"

"The Comanches?" Don Julio came back. "Oh, you mean

123

those Indian raiders." Don Julio smiled condescendingly. "They might attack small places. But they would never venture against a strong establishment like Vega Verde.

"If they would be that fool-hardy, we would call in the men from our outlying ranches and we would destroy them. We have cloe to one hundred of the finest vaqueros in Nueva Vizcaya."

Padre Leon wanted to feel more confident with Don Julio as a new-found ally who did not fear the Comanche. But certain observations of his own did not jibe with Don Julio's remarks.

He had seen few cattle in the hills, even though rich green grass was visible. Few horses were in the corral when Don Julio brought his sorrel to the barn. Few retainers worked around the establishment.

Yet when the two sat down to dinner, the elegance of the table showed no evidence of decline. The fowl was an exquisite partridge. Don Julio chose from a wide selection of excellent wines. Yet Padre Leon noticed that only one woman worked in the large kitchen. He presumed that she was the wife of the man who served.

When Padre Leon thanked his host and prepared to take his leave, Don Julio sent his overseer as a companion.

When the two had ridden a safe distance, his companion began: "I heard what Don Julio said to you, mi padre. What he said was true twenty years ago. This hacienda was the finest in the valley of the Conchos."

Padre Leon said nothing.

"Golden Lance has hit one after another of our outlying ranches. The best of our breeding stock has been driven off. All but a few of the most loyal retainers have fled for safety with their families. I cannot blame them. I cannot stop them.

"I have tried to tell Don Julio. But he is like a tortoise with his head pulled into its shell, or like a child who covers his ears so as not to hear what he does not want to hear. He lives in the memory of what was."

They rode out of the gap into the valley of the Conchos.

"Life was hard for Don Julio when his wife died. She was a strong woman, who faced facts with a level eye. We had hoped the daughter Dona Donosa would be like her. And she is! But when she brought back that reckless husband of hers, we knew night was coming. He did not possess that air of responsibility which went with being patron of a large hacienda. The open country was not for him. He and Donosa went back south."

Disgust had been in his voice as he spoke of the son-in-law. But now he said in full pride, "Don Julio was never a great man; but at least he carried himself in a manner fitting his position."

The overseer paused, then continued almost as an afterthought: "We no longer number our cattle in the thousands, but in the hundreds. We do not have one hundred vaqueros, we have at most ten. If Golden Lance comes our way, it is the end."

Padre Leon felt the overseer's deep warmth of affection for Don Julio. _He_ _will_ _stay_ _with_ _the_ _old_ _man_ _till_ _the_ _end_, he concluded.

"John XXIII"
sermon

Just the other day, I read this incident in the life of good Pope John. He had served for some years as Nuncio of the Holy Father in Bulgaria. Pope Pius XII had decided to assign him to a new post.

As Archbishop Roncalli, the man who was to become Pope John, left Sofia, the capital of Bulgaria, he gave these farewell words to the people among whom he had lived:

"Wherever I may go in the world, anyone from Bulgaria who might be in distress and who comes to my house at night will find a candle lit in my window. He has only to knock and the door will be opened to him whether he be Catholic or Orthodox. 'A brother from Bulgaria', this will be title enough. He will find the most affectionate hospitality."

Affectionate hospitality was what Archbishop Roncalli promised. Affectionate hospitality, he gave. Wherever he served God's people, in Turkey, in France, in Venice, in Rome, this loving approachability came to be the most significant feature of his personality. When he became pope, everyone in the world came to feel that if they had a problem -- whatever it might be -- they could go to Pope John and he would understand.

Pompous and formal individuals tended to think of this "loving approachability" as a quirk of His Holiness, something not quite fitting for a Sovereign Pontiff, and out of character with his more proper predecessors. Had they read their gospels with open minds, they would have seen that this was the most distinctive feature of Christ whom Pope John served.

125

A PRIEST FOR ALL REASON

We have just heard Saint Luke's account of the first Christmas. The Son of God has become man. God has entered into the course of man's life not by messages of the prophets, or warnings in the storm or earthquake, but by coming among us. Emmanuel -- God with us... "In the fullness of time, God sent His Son, born of woman, born under the law, that He might redeem those who are under the law...that we might have the adoption of sons."

And what is the most significant fact of His coming -- simplicity, yes, poverty, almost destitution, yes -- but even more striking, a loving approachability...The shepherd from the hills, the least of the children of Israel, come running to greet him. The door of the cave is open...Christ was never to dwell behind locked doors...always accessible...always lovingly approachable...With Christ, the candle is always lit in His window...We may come to Him at any time... anyone may come!

This, then, is our Christmas wish to you...that you always remember Christ has a candle lit in His window...for you...

"DOUG X"
previously unpublished

Doug Hegker talked himself into my life just before the Kennedy-Nixon election of 1960. That night, as on many Tuesdays and Thursdays during the winter, I had been enjoying a pleasant evening of ice-skating at the Winter Garden. Shortly after ten, I was taking off my skates, preparing to drive home. Suddenly, a harsh challenging voice blurted out: "Kennedy doesn't have a chance. There are too damned many bigots in this country."

I looked up at the speaker. He was slightly dissipated in appearance, about thirty years old, of moderate build, close to six feet tall, of light complexion. The room went silent. I glanced at those around me. Of the twenty people in the room, the fellow with whom I had driven to the rink that night was a general Christian. Big George was Jewish, Frannie a Catholic. The rest of the people I didn't know. Wanting to avoid ill feeling, I said sharply, "I'll match that Nixon money."

"Go at him, Father," Frannie shouted.

George added, "Yeah, let him have it, Father."

The man turned: "Are you a priest?" he asked.

While he was trying to readjust to the situation, I

126

said simply, "Yes, I am. I'll match any of that money you want to put on Richard Nixon."

I looked squarely at his slightly dissipated face. "I believe that there are just as many Eisenhower people in the big cities who will vote for Senator Kennedy for religious reasons, as there are Democrats in rural areas who will vote against him because he is a Catholic."

"I don't want to bet any money on Nixon", the man answered, with careful reflection. "By the way", he interjected, "I'm Doug Hegker." Then he blurted out: "you know something -- I hope Kennedy wins." Then he abruptly changed the subject -- "Do you have a ride home?"

"Yes, I do have a ride home, thank you," I said. "Maybe some other time." I rose and left.

It rained in St. Louis early in the evening of the election. I remember distinctly. I was at a testimonial dinner at the Gray Ghost Restaurant. I momentarily forgot Doug Hegker and the Nixon money that wasn't there.

Two nights later, the phone rang. "Doug Hegker here, Father -- would you like to go skating tonight?"

"Fine", I said. "Where did you plan on going?"

"I'd like to go to Steinberg's," he said -- "I prefer skating outdoors, if you don't mind".

"Okay with me".

The Steinberg Rink in Forest Park was the gift of Mrs. Mark Steinberg in memory of her husband. It was spacious and ordinarily not too crowded on a weekday night. (Every weekend, however, the small fry skaters proved once again that there was a population explosion.)

Nothing particularly unusual happened that night -- for Doug, that is. While skating with an attractive young lady, for no apparent reason he left her in the middle of the ice. Seeing me, he came over and said with disgust: "You know something. That girl is a nurse." His tone suggested that he thought she belonged among the untouchables.

"That's fine," I said.

"No, that's not fine," he shot back.

"What's wrong with being a nurse?" I asked.

"Well, they belong to the health professions. They're affiliates of the AMA. I'm a working man. And the AMA is against working men." His vehemence approached violence. "The AMA spends hundreds of thousands every year to put through right-to-work laws. They're against me. I'm a working man, see?"

"Doug", I said, "nurses are probably the least paid people in the whole health professions. Certainly they do

127

not have anything to do with the policies of the AMA." I began to realize that talking to Doug was like arguing with a computer. But I went on anyway. If I could not convince him, at least he would know I never agreed with him.

"I was spiritual director of nursing students for four years in Denver. At the beginning of each year, the director of nursing education would give me a list of first year students with residence, age, previous school, occupation of their fathers. Most of their fathers worked with their hands. They were miners. They drove bulldozers. They fixed machines. They owned small farms." I paused, looked at him and went on, "Nurses are people, good people. Now you get this silly idea out of your head."

The laugh was on me. Doug did not get that silly idea or any silly idea out of his head.

A few nights later just before 6 o'clock, Doug called again. I soon got to realize that Doug always would call at 5 to 6. It so happened that, at the time, dinner began at 20 to 6. Thus I would be right in the middle of the meal when Doug's call would come in. "You going skating tonight?" he asked, completely dispensing with any introduction. I told him that I planned on going to the Winter Garden that evening. The weather didn't look good.

"I plan to go to Steinberg; I like it outside. But I'll be glad to take you over to the Winter Garden."

"Okay", I readily agreed.

He was already coming twelve blocks out of his way to get me; and now he was going to drive six minutes beyond where he was going to take me to the Winter Garden. But it didn't seem to bother Doug. He drove into the side alley at 7:15. He began like a continued story with no resume of earlier chapters. "I met a girl out at the rink the other night," he began. "She seemed to be a real nice girl. And, do you know what I found out? I found out she was a nurse."

"Lucky for you, Doug -- nurses are like people -- good, bad, and indifferent. In fact, I think the greater percentage of them are among the better people that you'll ever meet."

"But they're affiliates of the AMA."

"Yeah, I heard that before, and I denied it before."

"Well, you know something? The AMA is against the working man, and I'm a mechanic, and I'm going to finish up my course at Bailey Tech pretty soon; and who's against me, well, I'm against."

One might wonder why Doug was running into so many nurses, but if he knew that the Steinberg Rink was within easy walking distance of three of the largest nursing schools in Missouri and three of the largest and finest hospitals in the state also, he would understand that it is not surprising that a fair percentage of these young ladies would be nurses. I often wondered if the name of Doug Hegker ever came up at the perennial bull session on third south just before the evening shift gave way to the night nurses. If it had, what an interesting recording it would have made!

Doug still had that slightly dissipated look which seemed to be a part of him and in no way dependent on bourbon, confinement or late hours. He could skate two hours on a lovely evening and he looked just as he did when a gloomy driving rain forced him off the ice after one turn around the rink.

The next night he decided to go to the Winter Garden. When I came in after fifteen minutes of skating, Doug was talking to Frannie. From Frannie's point of view, this wasn't surprising. She's a friend of all the world. Tall and thin, she was a skating champ a few years back. When she's on that ice, she simply flies. No expenditure of effort, no energy used, like Major White off in space. You begin to wonder where that powerful drive is coming from, but with no effort at all she just goes much faster than anybody.

Few men can keep up with Frannie; in fact, when Frannie partner-skates, she usually pulls her partner along as he struggles to keep up. Only one fellow can really keep up with Frannie at her fastest. He's a handsome, sad-looking fellow who speeds around alone except for an occasional skate with Frannie. He seems to have some secret sorrow of his own.

Frannie's the one who organizes the picnics we have in the off-season when we're not skating. If there is to be anything special, she's the central intelligence behind the whole program.

If one knows Frannie, he soon knows everybody. In fact, when I came back from Denver in 1956 and went out to the Winter Garden to skate for the first time, I knew only the fellow I rode out with. He introduced me to Frannie. Soon I knew hundreds of people.

So it was not surprising that Doug would be talking to Frannie. What was more surprising was that she was a nurse.

When Frannie went back out on the ice to skate, I asked Doug, "How come you're talking to Frannie? Don't you know she's a nurse?"

"Well, she's different," he said.

I had to admit that that was true. Frannie is at least a little superior to the vast majority of people in any classification, whether nurses or otherwise.

A week later the phone rang. "You know something", Doug said for the fortieth time since I first met him a few weeks before -- "you know something."

"Oh, I know a few things," I said.

He went right on, regardless of my attempted pleasantry -- "Bobby Kennedy just doesn't like working men; he's out to get us."

"Who told you, George Meany?" I asked.

"First, it's Hoffa, then it's the rest of us -- he just doesn't like us."

"That would really be smart, for the Kennedys to turn against the laborer, wouldn't it?" I said. "They need the laboring people and the other big city vote to stay in power."

I spoke with no hope of convincing Doug. I had already long ago realized it was futile to try to convince him of anything. I simply wanted to clarify things in my own mind.

I began to realize, about this time, that while Doug carried on a monologue when he was with two, he carried on a dialogue when he was with more than two. One evening I was talking with Big George when Doug walked up. "You know Big George, don't you, Doug?"

"Yeah", he said, "Bobby Kennedy's trying to flatten us working people." He directed his words to me. I recognized the topic he had previously monologued in my ears on the way out. He did not direct a single thought to Big George. I really should say that he never even directed words to him. Big George was completely out of it, as far as Doug was concerned. But this time, at least, Doug would stop and wait for me to answer.

The next week I was out of town. But ten days later, Doug called again and came by. "You know something," he said, "I'm Prussian. And I've been reading that Prussians are pretty stubborn people. And I guess I just better be stubborn then."

"I don't think you really have to try very hard, Doug," I ventured. "I think you've gotten a head start." I hazarded a laugh, but he just kept that straight, tired look on his face and didn't think much about what I said. In fact, Doug was so busy thinking his own thoughts, he did not have much time to think about anything which another might suggest.

While Doug was still on this Prussian bend of his I saw

him out at the rink one night; he was standing with Big
George, all 265 lbs. of him, a star athlete from Soldan High
twenty-five years back; alongside was another 210 pounds of
muscle, and a third who was a good strapping 185 and built
like a Missouri blocking back in the days of Paul Christman.
All three of these fellows were of Jewish background. Any
one of the three could have remodelled Doug with one hand.

Doug saw me coming and blurted out, "Father, I have a
question. Don't you think Hitler did a lot for the working
people of Germany?"

"Doug", I said, pointing to the ice, "I think you ought
to show that nurse how to skate backwards."

I looked back at Big George and his two friends. They
just shook their heads. All I could remember at that moment
was what George had told me once before. "You know, Father," he had said, "We Jewish people don't believe in violence."

It was fortunate for Doug that the Jewish people as a
whole abhor violence, and that Big George, and his two
friends in particular, abhorred violence.

Big George had begun skating two years before, in spite
of weak ankles. As he'd set his long blades down on the ice
it sounded like Admiral Perry slashing his way with a dog
team and sled towards the North Pole. But Big George was
game and he was humble; and he was helped by the girls --
Frannie, especially, and a few more of them, all very good
skaters. He had hardly gotten started when he had a chance
to show how really humble he was. Someone asked if he would
like to be the clown in the skating show at the end of the
season. Big George said he'd be willing to make a try at
it.

When the night of the skating exhibition came, George
wore an oversize fluffy shirt such as a third grade girl
would wear to a party. After several fine exhibitions by
figure skaters, he went on the ice. Normally the clowns in
skating events, like those in rodeos, are experts who put on
a show of trying to stand up under unusual circumstances.
Most of the people in the audience did not know that George
was a beginner. When he started off across that ice, everyone was laughing. He headed for the wall. Two fellows
dashed out after him and caught him just before he hit the
wall. Few people in the audience knew that George actually
couldn't stop. Had it not been for the two experts he probably would have landed, all 265 lbs. of him, outside on
Delmar Boulevard. A second time, George charged across the
ice like a tackle on the Chicago Bears going down under a

131

punt. Joyous laughter of the crowd followed. The two good skaters plunged after him, saved the south wall of the Winter Garden from terrible disaster. After several other near-mishaps, operations came to a safe conclusion. The M.C. announced that, contrary to their expectations, George was not an expert skater clowning, but a beginning skater with a tremendous sense of fun. The applause was deafening.

Two nights later I was happily enjoying my meal. I had forgotten that it was almost 5 to 6. Suddenly the phone rang. It was my bell. "You know something?"

"Oh, I think I do, Doug", I said. "What's on your mind?"

"Did you see my picture in the paper?"

"I did."

"Well, what did you think of it?"

"Oh, I thought it was fine."

"Well, let me tell you -- this fellow Ted Nuze from the Post-Dispatch; he called up and he said, 'This is Ted Nuze at the Post. Your name Doug Hegker?' and I said, 'Yes, I'm Doug Hegker.' He said, 'Well, Mr. Hegker, you won the Irish sweepstakes.' 'Get off my back,' I said, and I hung up."

"What did you do that for, Doug? Don't you know Ted Nuze is one of the old hands down at the Post? He's been with them for many years."

"Well, how was I to know? This guy says, 'I'm Ted Nuze at the Post'. Another says, 'I'm Joe Lyon at the zoo' -- another, 'I'm Bill Sands at the beach.' Well, I'm tired after a hard day's work. And I thought it was some guy out at Steinberg trying to give me a hard time.

"Then the phone rings again and the same voice said, 'Mr. Hegker, if you don't believe I'm Ted Nuze, why don't you just call the Post-Dispatch and then ask for Ted Nuze at Station 342?'

"I said, 'Okay.' So I did just that. I hung up and I dialed the Post. I asked for Station 342 and I got this fellow Ted Nuze and he told me again that I won the Irish Sweepstakes. While he's talking, I'm thinking: 'That's nice -- I could certainly use about five grand.' He goes on, 'Mr. Hegker, you've won $150,000.'

"I said: 'Get off my back,' and I hung up again.

"A few minutes later, the phone rings again. 'Mr. Hegker, this is Ted Nuze. I'd like you to listen for a few minutes; could I send a photographer out and get your picture?"

"'Can you take my dog's picture too?' I said."

"'Okay, we'll take you and the dog and anybody else you

want. But we want to get this story.' So he and the photographer came out. But they didn't put the dog's picture in the paper."

"Okay, Doug", I said. "The dog will just have to wait. Doug, I think you ought to go to Ireland, now."

"Well, what do I want to go to Ireland for?"

"Go over to Ireland and invest the money."

"Well, that's a good idea; you know, the government's going to take quite a bit of it in taxes."

"You go to Ireland -- you take your mother along and stay awhile. Maybe you might want to buy a castle and be a Duke or something and live over there."

"Well, I don't know about that," he came back, but he didn't seem sure.

Two nights later the phone rang at 5 to 6. "You know something? The government's going to take over $100,000 of my money."

"Well, that still leaves you $50,000 more than you had last week."

"Yeah, but $100,000 is a lot of money."

"But $50,000 is more than what you had before and is still a lot of money."

"I think I'm going to go to Ireland."

"You go to Ireland," I said.

Three or four nights later Doug was back at the rink again. Everyone congratulated Doug. It all seemed a big joke. Nobody really took it seriously, except Doug himself. He said that four girls he had jilted during the past two years had called him up to renew old friendships. Before his Irish thoroughbred came home first, I had seen only one girl skate with Doug more than once. She was a Spanish girl from Carondelet. She was still friendly but the rest still seemed to keep their asthetic distance at all times. It was the same now.

Several weeks later I received a postal card from Ireland with my name simplified and one of the words misspelled. The next card came from London. It had no message whatsoever, so no other word besides my name was misspelled. The third came from Germany -- no message. A fourth card came from Italy, no message.

Not long afterward Big George and I were sitting at the side of the rink after the session was over. "Father," he said, "Your friend Doug was out at the Steinberg last night. He just got back from Europe. He's flashing $20 bills as if they were dimes; that fellow's crazy."

"Give him time," I said, "give him time."

"Just give him time," George retorted, "and somebody'll stick those $20 bills down his throat and strangle him if he doesn't shut up."

At 5 to 6 the following night an old familiar voice began, "You know something?"

"How was your European trip?" I interruped. "Great. You know something?" "Kennedy is selling out to the Africans. Just let me tell you -- the Africans are taking over this country. There's no question; that's just it."

More debating practice. I began, "I notice that the southern Senators balked at Kennedy's proposal to set up a department of urban welfare simply because he was going to put a Negro in charge of it. It doesn't look to me as if things are overbalanced in favor of the Negro."

"Well, let me tell you. The white man's day is over. You can be sure that the Africans are in."

All during the long winter after President Kennedy was shot, Doug continued on his anti-African binge. He sounded like a grand kleagle of the Ku Klux Klan, a Southern Governor and Senator Bilbo all wrapped up in one. Every single cliche ever brought up in the whole history of race relations he mouthed at some time or other as if it were a new original thought which he had just discovered. "We ought to send all the Africans back to Africa. I don't want them living next door to me. I ain't got nothing against Africans, BUT ...... there are good Africans like there are good other people, BUT ......"

About this time Malcolm X moved into the headlines, raving on the left as irrationally as Doug did on the right.

"Here comes Doug X", Frannie said one evening at the rink.

He did not say hello. Just off like a rocket from the newly re-named Cape Kennedy launching pad, he began, "I had hopes when Lyndon Johnson became president, but I find things are just as bad as when Kennedy was president. The Africans are taking over this country. You just mark my words. Johnson sold out; that's all there is to it; he just sold clean out."

One evening as the winter season was slowly giving way to spring Doug asked, "You want to go roller skating sometime?"

Just to pursue a more pleasant subject than Africans or his few other pet subjects, I said, "Yes, I guess I'll go. You give me a ring sometime". Thereupon I forgot about it.

One cool night during the summer, my phone rang at 5 to 6. "You know something? We ought to go out to Steinberg

134

tonight."

I needed a little exercise. Even though I never particularly cared for roller skating, I had more or less agreed. So I said, "Okay." An hour later, Doug was down in a brand new convertible of some kind or other that suggested his new financial status. Off we went for Forest Park and the Steinberg, transformed now into a roller skating rink. While few Negroes seem to care for outdoor winter sports, they certainly like to roller skate. Many of them seemed skilled at it. When we got to the Steinberg there were two hundred Negro skaters and no white people there.

Doug and I intergrated the skating rink. As we put on our skates, he joshed with one of the rink custodians.

Doug laughed, put our equipment in the locker, and we started for the rink.

"Hey, Tom," he said to the first boy we met, "I want you to meet Father. Father, this is Tom."

We talked to Tom a little while, and pretty soon Doug introduced me to some else. One of the custodians, a Negro boy of nineteen, skated up.

"Hi, Governor Wallace", he began.

"Okay, Martin Luther King," Doug shot back, "You can't convert me." The pleasantries went on for a few minutes.

Before the evening was over, Doug had introduced me to sixteen of his friends -- all "Africans." I tried to reconcile this with Doug's strictures on their taking over the country. They certainly had taken over the Steinberg Rink. During the entire evening only three other Caucasians came.

When the sessions were over and we got in the car, the sight of his new red-trimmed convertible recalled to Doug his new status. "You know, we property owners got no chance in this country. Labor and the Africans are taking away our liberty. In just a few years, you watch it, you want to hire somebody, you can't hire the one you want. You want to live somewhere, you can't live where you want to. You gotta belong to a minority group; you gotta hire who they want you to hire.

"Who's they?" I said.

"You gotta hire who they want you to hire," he repeated, "and you gotta live where they want you to live, and with whom they want you to live; there's just no freedom left."

I was out of town the next month or two and pretty soon the ice-skating had begun again. In the meantime the Winter Garden had been torn down after all those years. It had been put up back in 1904. It had been a spacious ice-pal-

135

ace. This year Saint Louis was going to have a new one.
The same people ran it.

At 5 to 6 one night in early November the phone rang.
I lifted the receiver.

"You know something? I want to join either the States'
Rights Party or Nazi Party; I haven't made up my mind
which."

"I think that either idea is absolutely idiotic," I
answered. "So it hardly makes much difference which one you
join."

One nice clear night in winter - it was warm and bright, I went out to the Steinberg. There was Doug. "Did you
see the picture of these nuns walking with Martin Luther
King down in Selma, Alabama? What's the church coming to?
Do I belong to this organization?"

"I don't think you do, as a matter of fact," I responded. "How long has it been since you've been to church?"

"Well, I don't believe in that sort of thing...."

I said, "You didn't go last Christmas -- you didn't go
the Christmas before. You haven't been as long as I've
known you. You haven't been to church once."

"Well, let me tell you, what's the Cardinal doing sending a delegate down there to have these demonstrations. We
have enough trouble with these Africans without the church
butting into this thing."

Three nights later, at 5 to 6: "You know something?
I'm gonna leave; the church is just taking everybody's
money. They're gonna take my money."

"Has anybody ever asked you for your money?" I asked.
"Did I ever ask you for a quarter?"

"No."

"Well, then what makes you think they're gonna take
it?"

"Well, that's the way they are."

"The way who are? Who's they?"

"Well, I'm just gonna quit the church anyway."

"Did you tell Pope Paul?" I asked.

"You gotta tell him?" he came back.

Not long after this, I was talking to Big George.
Frannie came up. "Did you hear that Doug X is going to
leave the country?" she asked. When we shook our heads,
she went on. "He's going to live in the Black Forest."

"That's good," Big George said, "the blacker, the
better!"

A few nights later we were sitting dunking doughnuts.

"Did you hear what happened to Doug?" Big George asked.

"He got his face smashed in. He was out shooting his mouth off about how bad the country was getting to be and he was going to join the Nazi party and go over to Germany to live, and some fellow took enough, got fed up and he remodeled him right then and there."

"One of your boys, George?" I asked.

"No, no, Father, we don't believe in violence, even with a man like Doug."

"One of his African friends?" Frannie asked. Big George shook his head again. "I thought maybe it'd be some Slavic fellow or an anti-Nazi German who spent some time in a concentration camp," Big George said. "But not at all. It was a German, some guy that fought on the Russian front for four years of the war, came over here afterwards. Kind of think he felt he was making amends for fighting in Hitler's wars. He walked up to Doug and said, 'Fella, you're nuts. I was over there; I was on Hitler's team; I admit it, but I'm not proud of it. Everything Hitler said was sheer nonsense. And everything you say is sheer nonsense. Now you shut up.'"

"But Doug didn't believe in shutting up. So this fellow let him have it."

It was a good thing that I heard this story. It made me just a little bit more ready (not that I would have ever really been ready) for the call that came at 5 to 6 a week later. "You know something." It had been years since Doug had ever introduced himself or said hello.

"Doug," I said, "I know lots of things."

"Well, let me tell you -- this country's gettin' better every day. They're givin' everybody a chance; they're givin' the working man a chance. They're givin' the African people a chance. Even the AMA doesn't have it so bad."

"I met this fellow the other day who'd fought for Hitler. He really knew what the score was."

"Persuasive fellow?" I asked.

"Yes! Had real convincing arguments."

"That's what I heard!"

Doug went right on. "We'll have to do a little something about stopping these states rights party people and the Nazi party people. They ain't many of them, but we gotta stop them anyway, and people like some of those southern Governors. But you know, people like you and me, we want to make something of this country. And I think we will."

"You know something, Doug", I said, "you know something? I just been thinking back. You still owe me an election bet. Kennedy won in 1960, you remember?"

137

A PRIEST FOR ALL REASON

"A French Nun With An American Dream"
from Catholics in America

Philippine Duchesne had an unusual kind of man trouble on her arrival in the American Mid-west. She had to deal with two zealous but unpredictable clergymen: Bishop Louis W. V. Du Bourg, who had invited her to America; and Jesuit Superior Charles Felix Van Quickenborne, her reluctant spiritual director. Without understanding something of these totally different personalities, one cannog grasp the difficulties Mother Duchesne faced in setting up the first convent of the Religious of the Sacred Heart outside of France, and the first free school west of the Mississippi.

A colonial aristocrat educated in Paris, Du Bourg felt more at home dining with President Washington than running a frontier diocese. Rugged Van Quickenborne found his place riding the mission trails or moving up the wild Missouri. A flamboyant promoter, Du Bourg could enlist many missionaries for the new world, but never stopped to think how they would feed, house or clothe themselves. The more practical Van Quickenborne took up his axe and led his Jesuit novices into the forests to build their own log cabin novitiate.

Du Bourg had promised Mother Duchesne that the nuns could begin a school in Saint Louis, the future metropolis of the Midwest; but sent her to the then thriving but eventually quiet town of St. Charles, Missouri twenty miles west-northwest of Saint Louis. He promised that the Jesuit Superior would serve as the nuns' spiritual director; but neglected to notify Van Quickenborne, who had little expertise and less relish for the unexpected assignment. Van Quickenborne gave Mother Duchesne little support in her difficult work...

But first, who was Philippine Duchesne?

The daughter of a prosperous and progressive lawyer in lovely Grenoble, gateway to the French Alps, she grew up in a changing world. She was born in late August 1769, just two weeks to a day after Napoleon. France was losing her colonial empire. The government could not handle acute financial crises, while a group of widely-read writers -- Voltaire, Rousseau, among others -- called for drastic change. Her father, Pierre-Francois Duchesne worked for reform.

When she was twelve, Philippine went to a boarding school in Grenoble conducted by the Visitation nuns. Spiritual director Pere Aubert often told the girls of his experiences among the Indians in America. Philippine decided she wanted to be a nun-missionary. Hearing of this wild dream, her father took her out of the convent school, and set about arranging a suitable marriage. Headstrong and independent, Philippine said "No" to several prospective suitors and, at the age of 19, joined the Visitandines.

Her father was unhappy with her; but soon the French Revolution absorbed all his energies. When the government turned violent, he took his family to their country home. The Extremist regime closed the convent; and soon Philippine rejoined her family. Later when the Reign of Terror ended, she returned to Grenoble to work among the poor and the orphaned. Two Visitandines and several nuns from other congregations gathered about her. Always willing to do the difficult herself, she expected others to do the same. When she could not reopen the old Visitation convent, she and her group joined the new congregation of the Religious of the Sacred Heart.

Philippine worked in Grenoble 11 years then went to Paris in 1815. Three years later she heard Bishop Du Bourg speak of the American West, and appealed successfully to the mother foundress, Madeline Sophie Barat. With three other nuns, Philippine sailed from Bordeaux for New Orleans. Then she took the steamboat Franklin up the Mississippi to Saint Louis in the Territory of Missouri. The first steamboat had reached the frontier town only two years before.

In France, Bishop Du Bourg had led her to believe she could open a school for girls in Saint Louis. Several prosperous French families wanted them do do so. But Bishop Du Bourg had her locate in St. Charles on the Missouri, with a promotional speech that anticipated the town's growth by a century and a half. Saint Louis had more immediate needs: a resident pastor and a new church to replace the caved-in ramshackle cabin that had sagged for almost fifty years. A survey by Bishop Flaget of Kentucky several years before had showed Saint Louis the least religious of the French communities in the area.

The school in Saint Charles barely lasted through the first hard winter. A year later, the nuns moved across the Missouri to a French farm community called Florissant. After four years there, Mother Duchesne welcomed two Jesuit priests and seven seminarians who came west to open a combined Indian school and Jesuit seminary. Father Van Quickenborne gave little spiritual guidance to the nuns, but Mother Duchesne made lasting friendships with several seminarians who would later on help her fulfill her missionary dreams of working among the Indians.

With the arrival of the Indian boys at the Jesuit seminary, several of their sisters joined the other students
from Saint Louis and Southeast Missouri who attended the
nuns' school. As several American-born candidates joined
Mother Philippine's little band, she opened four convents
and two schools in west central Louisiana. Supported by the
prosperous French-speaking plantation owners, these schools
succeeded in the Bayou area, while the Florissant foundation
staggered along. Although vicar, she did not interfere with
the internal affairs of the Louisiana convents.

Shortly after Joseph Rosati, the Vincentian Superior,
succeeded Bishop Du Bourg in 1827, he invited Mother Philippine to open a school in Saint Louis. On May 2 of that
year she came into the city to start classes in a building
donated by a prosperous immigrant business man, John Mul-
lanphy. After a few years, a younger nun succeeded Mother
Duchesne as head of the American venture. Superiors had not
found it easy to remove from office a dedicated woman, who
happened to be a first cousin of the Prime Minister of
France, Casimir Perier. But the change had to come. Mother
Duchesne went back to Florissant and engaged in a variety of
charitable activities.

During the ensuing decade, two of the Jesuit novices
she had befriended on their arrival at Florissant in 1823,
Peter Verhaegen and Peter Jan De Smet, had gone far: Verhaegen as president of Saint Louis University and Superior
of the Missouri Jesuit Mission; and Peter Jan De Smet as
missionary among the Indians farther West. The latter told
Mother Duchesne that the tribesmen needed nuns to teach religion to their daughters. She told him to see the new Superior in Louisiana. He did so, and won permission for nuns
to go west. No one mentioned Mother Duchesne. She was
weak, and seventy years old. But she had dreamed of working
among the Indians, and as yet had no chance to fulfill that
dream. Now the chance came. Peter Verhaegen arranged to
make his official visitation of the Jesuit Potawatomi Mission at such time as to accompany Mother Duchesne to Kansas.

She lived in an Indian hut all summer. Fortunately, a
log house was ready by winter but it had no fireplace and
only a ladder to sleeping quarters in the loft. She visited
the sick and elderly; and responded with a smile when the
children greeted her, since she had little facility with the
Potawatomi tongue. After one year in Kansas, superiors recalled her to St. Charles where they had built a new school
and convent. Prayer had consumed lots of her spare moments,
and sometimes whole nights, even during her busiest years.

Now she had plenty of time for prayer, for writing letters to relatives and nuns in France, and for mending clothes for the girls in the school. Brought up in class-conscious French society, she had always dealt formally with adults; but children found her easy to approach. She also had the fortunate presence of her dear friend Father Verhaegen as pastor of the parish. He gave her Viaticum on November 18, 1852, and in his funeral statement two days later spoke of her sanctity.

She had seen Missouri grow from a frontier territory into the largest state of the West. The editors of the Dictionary of American Biography recognized her contribution to the building of the state and the nation, one of the few contemporary women of the Trans-Mississippi region so honored. The Church beautified her in 1940.

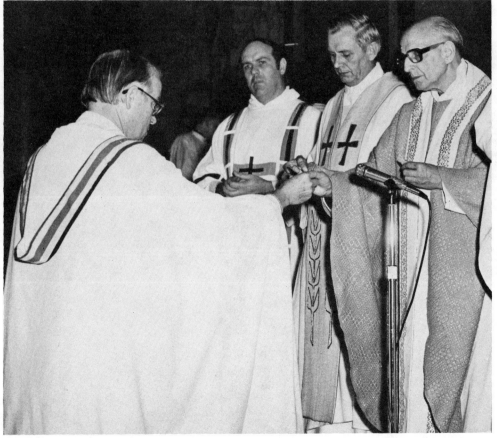

Father Faherty renews his vows before Jesuit Superior General Pedro Arrupe at the St. Francis Xavier Church in St. Louis. Fifty American Jesuits participated.

For Father Faherty, the church is people. Here he celebrates with girls from the Queen of Heaven Home after their
graduation from eighth grade.

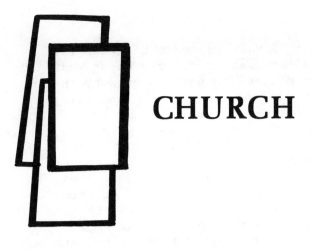

CHURCH

The Church -- its nature, its goals, its
people -- provide Barnaby Faherty with one of the
major topics in his writing. And, as in much of
his other writing, he brings the historian's perspective and the people-lover's personal concern.
He puts the Church, always, in the context of time
and studies its growth and worries over its struggles. For him, the Church is a missionary which
brings comfort to scattered souls. Perhaps this
vision comes from his intense interest in the
places in which he has lived -- particularly the
Rockies, Kansas, and St. Louis -- the latter a city
Catholic from its very beginnings as a trading
post on the Mississippi, and the former two objectives of the early missionary work. But whether the subject is, in fact, the missionary work
of the Church or the fictional treatment of a
priest's crisis of vocation in the changing
Church, this vision holds.

Four selections, two historical, one personal
experience, and one fictional, show some of the
products of his curiosity about and respect for
the institution that has provided the central direction in his life. The first selection, part of
the introduction to The Catholic Ancestry of St.
Louis, outlines Father Faherty's view of the role
of the Catholic Church in the development of the
special flavor of the city. In the second, from

an article entitled "Jesuit Pioneers Set Pace for Kansas' Church," we see Father Faherty doing what he loves to do, examining the parts played by individuals in the establishment of something greater than themselves. The Kansas Jesuits worked in a place that was not exactly hostile, but could perhaps be called indifferent to their contributions. Father Faherty shows us his Church working because of the individuals he describes. The story, "Learn from the Fig Tree," is one from a group of stories in which Barnaby Faherty explored what was happening to the Church in America after Vatican II from the perspective of priests caught up in the change. "Fig Tree" provides us with a character, a man about to leave the priesthood because he has forgotten that the Church is about people, clearly Father Faherty's view. In the last selection, from "A Visit to Utah," he takes the reader along on a visit to a monastery in Utah, hardly a citadel of Catholicism. But this piece is not just "My Day at the Monastery"; it is a picture of the people of the church living Christ's Word -- being the Church. He shows these men, cut off from much of the world, as people involved in the world in a truly Christian way.

For Father Faherty, the Church is an institution, yes, but it is an institution that rests in its people, whether nameless earlier settlers in St. Louis or authors published throughout the world.

from The Catholic Ancestry of St. Louis

The French founders of Saint Louis gave to the city a distinct and enduring Catholic spirit. During the forty years before it became a city of the United States, few members of other denominations resided here. When Saint Louis became American, members of various religious affiliations arrived. But even twenty years later they did not collectively outnumber the Catholics.

The friendly spirit of the original residents and the cooperation which marked their relationships with the newcomers explains the easy-going, happy attitude toward life in Saint Louis. Only two periods of strong inter-faith tension struck the city: one provoked by the Know-Nothings before the Civil War; the other stirred by the American Protective Association in the Nineties. These were merely passing phases in an otherwise peaceful community.

At times members of other faiths outnumbered the Catholic inhabitants of the city. But the preponderance was never marked for any great length of time. In his book, Inside U.S.A., social observer John Gunther wrote categorically that Saint Louis was a "Catholic city." A European observer made the startling statement that the cities of Saint Louis and New Orleans had the longest record without persecution of Catholics by irreligious governments of any Catholic cities in the western world. When one realizes that martyrs died in Paris, Dublin, and Madrid for their Catholic Faith, when even Rome itself went through periods of harsh anti-Catholic rule, this two hundred year record becomes even more significant.

The spirit of Saint Louis has always been as placid as the waters of the Mississippi in late summer. Sometimes it has seemed too relaxed, even sociologically unconcerned. Yet Saint Louis Catholics have led the dioceses and archdioceses of the world, not only proportionally but numerically, in contributions to the Christian missions. Several years ago one dollar of every fifteen given to the Propagation of the Faith throughout the entire world came from the Archdiocese of St. Louis. When one recalls that the Catholic population of the Archdiocese of Saint Louis is less than that of more than forty archdioceses and dioceses in the world, this becomes even more amazing.

from "Jesuit Pioneers Set Pace for Kansas Church"
Eastern Kansas Register
Anniversary Issue, 1977

A recent history of Kansas omits the word "Jesuit" from the Index. It fails to list the names of John Schoenmakers, the missionary, or Paul Ponziglione, the circuit-rider, or Francis Finn, the leading Catholic juvenile story teller of his time.

Was this an oversight? Not necessarily. Was it an example of prejudice, or bigotry or anti-Jesuit feeling typical of the Ku Klux days? Possibly - but the oddmakers would go slow.

Kansas has always been predominantly Protestant in population in outlook and in spirit. The state's pre-eminent editor, William Allen White, spoke of a "transplanted New

A PRIEST FOR ALL REASON

England conscience." Through much of its history Kansas has
reflected the spirit of colonial Puritan New England more
than present-day Rhode Island or Vermont do. Strong islands
of Catholicity stood out prominently in several sections of
what was a Protestant lake. But islands do not make a lake.

Jesuits did much in the Sunflower state. But most of
these efforts missed the mainstream of Kansas life. The
pioneer missionaries tried to make Christians of the Osage
and Potawatomi -- not exactly the swing votes even in Pop-
ulist days. One of their number wrote books that Catholic
boys in Belgium and the Rhineland read during two genera-
tions. But Protestant boys in Topeka had never heard of
"Tom Playfair" or "Harry Dee," just as the Catholic in Ellis
County may have missed "In His Steps." During 40 years of
this century Jesuits staffed one of the influential theological faculties of the country. But the science prof at
K-State hardly knew of this divinity school scarcely 30
minutes away at St. Marys.

The missionaries to the Osage and the Potawatomi have
struck their tepees. The once popular boarding high school
and college at St. Marys gave way in 1931 to the Depression
and the Missouri Jesuit Province's need of space for a
theologate. After 40 years that Theological Faculty departed for a big city university campus. The short-lived
Kapaun High School in Wichita said good-by to its Jesuit
staff. Only a few individual Jesuits still work in the
state. After almost a century and a half of religious
activities the Jesuits have withdrawn entirely from Kansas
borders. They had their part in Kansas Catholic history --
and departed.

from "Learn From the Fig Tree"
previously unpublished

"The Weather Bureau at Lambert-St. Louis International
Airport has issued a storm warning for Ste. Genevieve, Perry, and Cape Girardeau Counties in Southeast Missouri, and
Monroe, Randolph and Jackson Counties in Southwestern Illinois. Spotters in widely scattered areas of Missouri have
reported sighting funnel clouds. The storm is moving in a
north-easterly direction. This warning will be in effect
for the next two hours. Dan Pana reporting for station WRTH
in Wood River. Our next news cast will be at 1:55 p.m." . .
On any other day of the year, Father "Ves" Baden would
have turned back on the Great River Road below Chester, Illi-

146

nois and raced for the safety of home. But this was the
only afternoon he could drive up to Ruma, and see his friend
Father Tom Meath. He wanted to talk over the message that
he received from Rome. He dreaded the thought of that thick
envelope with the Rome postmark; yet he had spent several
years thinking about the matter before he had written for
permission to leave the priesthood. He would have to sign
the two documents and then return one to Rome. He had not
yet signed either. He hadn't even opened the envelope. It
wasn't an easy thing to do, to turn one's back on half a
lifetime and begin anew. He didn't know. Fortunately, he
could talk to Tom Meath once more. Tom had come down from
Chicago to take the place of the Pastor at the little town
of Ruma for the weekend. When Ves had first broached the
subject of leaving the priesthood several years before, Tom
suggested that he take a temporary leave of absence and work
for a doctorate in creative writing at the University of
Wisconsin. This he did. But still doubt filled his mind.
When Ves decided to ask for final leave, he relied on Tom to
attest to the sincerity of his request.

Strangely, Tom had more complaints with the Church than
he had, yet had no intention of renouncing his vocation.
Tom had always favored married clergy, and felt the Church
had lost immeasurably, especially in the Protestant parts of
the world, by not having a married as well as a celibate
clergy. Tom felt that little real brotherhood existed in
religious communities including their own. He felt that the
sociologists were right when they said at the time that
priests were beyond disillusionment with church leadership
in the United States.

Tom had admitted to Ves that certain men and women in
the religious life had gotten into a state of mind wherein
the only way to cease living a lie was to leave their congregations. But Tom's life was not a lie. He was successful in his apostolate even though he felt the superiors
restricted him greatly in the work that he could do. He had
a large group of people scattered around who relied on his
religious help. In fact, they looked upon him as an oak
standing in a storm. Above all, he had always felt that
Christ and His Church alone gave life any meaning.

How often as Ves and Tom had gone through the seminary
course together, Tom Meath had said: "To whom shall we go
but to You, Oh, Lord." Things might be bad; they might be
miserable; but they were not totally without meaning. Tom
had always insisted that amid all the peoples in the world,
in the last two thousand years, God had shown His loving

147

hand with none so intimately and intensely as with the
Christian people. This was Christ's Church. And Christ was
the Son of God.

Ves wished he could look at things as Tom did . . .

With the deft fingers of his left hand, Ves checked his
Roman collar to see that it had not twisted out of place.
As he did so, a sad look gripped his full handsome face -- a
face, his friends often said, that should have brought him
the monsignorial red. He realized that this would probably
be the last time he put on the Roman collar that he had worn
so proudly for twenty years. He did not dress in priestly
black on the campus of Southwestern University, where he had
been teaching for a full year after finishing his doctorate
in creative writing at the University of Wisconsin. To most
of the students, he was simply Dr. Sylvester Baden, Associate Professor of Creative Writing. When he notified the
Bishop of the area that he had accepted the position, the
Bishop had answered that Father Baden would have to become
part of the Newman Apostolate on the campus or not function
publicly as a priest during his work at the state institution. Ves had visited the Newman Center and found the operation so "far out" that he decided to get a little apartment of his own in the neighborhood and cease to exercise
the ministry within the diocese. On the other hand, his activities at the school had gone well.

His work consisted of a small amount of teaching, and
much creative writing and editing in the office that put out
all University brochures, magazines, and publications.

He loved the southern Illinois country. He liked to
walk out along Crab Orchard Lake in the fall when the geese
came in by the tens of thousands. As to his classes, he
always found two or three students whose enthusiasm would
carry them through the plodding work that learning to write
entailed.

As time went on, it became steadily clearer to him that
he could not go on with one foot in the Church and one foot
in a secular educational institution. He could not but feel
depressed that somehow or other the Church had no place for
him while the State gladly used his services in a constructive and creative way. . .

Ves swung off Highway 3 onto 165, the road that eventually led to Fort Chartres State Park. One half mile down
165, he turned left again into the parking lot alongside of
St. Patrick's Church. He opened the glove compartment and
took out the unopened envelope with the Rome postmark. He
beat the envelope against the dashboard for a moment or two

and then, without opening it, stuck it into his pocket. He walked up to the rectory door. Tom was there to meet him, tall, trim, sturdy, his deep black hair showing no touch of gray. Tom took Ves' hand in his accustomed strong grip.

"You've put on a little weight, Ves," Tom said. "Too much sitting. Too little tennis."

"I haven't found anyone at Southwestern who has your patience to put up with a duffer like me. But there are more important things to talk about than tennis."

"True enough, Ves. Come on in. The pastor's office is fairly comfortable. And no one will interrupt us." Tom motioned Ves to the seat behind the desk. He himself sat on a folding chair next to the south window.

"The letter finally came from Rome," Ves said.

"Did you sign it?" Tom asked.

"Not yet," Ves came back. "It was hard enough to put in the original application for leave," he said. "This is even harder. I haven't even opened the envelope."

"And it wasn't the easiest letter of approval that I ever had to write." Tom said. "I call them as I see them; I'm not much for Roman formalities." A frown crossed his craggy face. "I remember the first time I had to ask for a marriage dispensation for two friends, one a Catholic, the other a Presbyterian. I put down the reasons why I thought this marriage would be a good one; and incidently, it has been a good one," Tom said with insistence. "The Chancellor wanted me to put down that if the couple didn'tget a dispensation, I believed that they would go off and get a JP wedding. I told him, 'No, Monsignor, I don't believe that; and I can't sign such a statement.'"

"'Well, it would be so much easier to process it,' the Monsignor said. 'The Archbishop would push it through faster. It is just a formality.'"

"'Nothing I sign my name to is a formality,' I told him. And that was the way it was with your letter to Rome. I wrote it as I saw it, Ves. I told them they were losing a truly valuable priest. Maybe that's why it took so long."

"They all take long, Tom, unless the priest has already contracted a civil marriage. Then the dispensation comes through more easily."

"In that case," Tom said, "the Bishop himself would probably have the wedding ceremony to show his broad-mindedness."

"That's just it," Ves came back. I'm not thinking of getting married. I am just standing here where I've always been. The Church has moved out on me and the Congregation of John Carroll has moved on. They are not the outfits I signed up with years ago."

"We've gone over that many times," Tom said, calmly, leaning back in his chair, "and I grant every point that you make. But you are a man of forty-five; you've given twenty-five years of your life to the service of the Church. Let's face it, you can't carve out a new career for yourself now."

"The Congregation and the Church were not very interested that I carve out a career for myself when I was in it," Ves said, defensively but not belligerently. "The Superior would rather have the Lancaster publishing house go under as it did than that I get a chance to run it."

"That's right," Tom Meath said. "You published six pamphlets that sold over a half million copies; a book that Hollywood made into a movie; another book that a leading woman anthropologist reviewed favorably and another that went into two paperback reprints in various corners of the English-speaking world. And the Superior made an illiterate crony of his director of the Lancaster Publishing House."

"It took him a year and a half to run the place into bankruptcy," Ves came back.

"That long?" Tom said. "I thought he had it under in two months. But what did the Superior offer you?"

"Superintendent of Buildings at the Seminary. He suggested that I teach creative writing to the seminarians. But we don't have any seminarians."

"You would have made a splendid Superintendent of Buildings," Tom came back with a smile. "Abe Lincoln was a fine country lawyer. But by the time he was fifty-two, he stood ready for more than that."

"Southwestern Illinois University seems much more interested in what I can do than the Congregation of John Carroll. I enjoy my work there. The students seem to like my class. I have no kicks."

"No argument there," Tom Meath said. "Countless others have had the same experience. Many sisters were consistently ill at ease when they taught in the eighth grade at St. Procopius School. Now they are teaching the same grade at Millard Fillmore Junior High and things are reasonably good. They don't have to live twenty-four hours a day with the same faculty people. Perhaps the administration is better; perhaps we expect more of Sister Principal than Mister Principal -- but don't always get it. We rightly expect more of Cardinal Meehan than of Mayor Monahan."

"I'd vote for Monahan any day," Ves said.

"Ves, we joined the Congregation of John Carroll, we

150

had a healthy camaraderie both in work and in play that made for a religious family," Tom said. "Sometimes they routinized the get-togethers like a Prussian parade. But strangely those formal gatherings did serve a purpose."

"Now, Tom, all they do is hold endless meetings on 'building community' -- as if it were a magic thing that one conjured out of the sky. No one dares to say that the basic thing people need to do to form community is to be kind and thoughtful to one another; to have concern for another's work, his interests, his needs."

"I can't deny that, Ves."

"Long ago, Tom, when you said that the Church should have English in the Mass, I agreed. To read the scriptures in a language that the people did not understand made as little sense as Governor Horace Hinderhofer's monthly message to his constituents. But some priests have not been satisfied with the prescribed advances. They've changed other things too. In the old days I could give a sermon at the eight o'clock Mass and not worry that the priest would say the opposite at the ten. Tom, I'm not leaving the Congregation and the Church. The Church and the Congregation left me. I'm still where I was ten years ago. The old Church has lost its tradition, its dignity, its direction, perhaps even its meaning."

"I'll forget your last sentence, Ves. You really didn't mean it. But let's take a look at you and the Church. I know that the people who ran the congregation didn't give you a challenge to match with your skills and ability. But still, Ves, there are so many people whose way of life depends upon the fact that you are a priest, that you have helped them in countless retreats, sermons, writings and personal counselling." He paused. "I hate to see all this come to an end."

"Perhaps I should have stayed as Assistant Chaplain at the Orphanage, where I was, right after ordination," Ves said meditatively. "Then I always felt there were youngsters who needed me. Even the girls who tried prostitution for a while later on, would write me at Christmas, promising to say their rosary once in a while and to be good girls the following year. But that's long over." He paused a moment then blurted out: "But what I can't understand, Tom, is that you have far more complaints about the Church than I have. And I'm the one who wants to leave."

"The Church means more to you in many ways, Ves, than to me. At least it means something different."

"I'm not convinced, Tom, but I'm listening."

151

"You were totally committed to the Church as an institution. You served it faithfully. It didn't respond. It rejected you, like last year's gear thrown out of this year's car."

"And aren't you committed to the Church, Tom?"

"Not committed in that way, Ves."

"Well, how are you committed, then?" Ves' voice was intense. His tone searching.

Tom Meath answered slowly, measuring every word. "I'm not committed to the Church as an organization, an instrument, a functioning mechanism. I'm committed to it as Christ living among us. I'm serving Christ through the Church -- not serving the organization in itself."

"And you're telling me that I was not committed to Christ, but to a mechanism that found me a replacable gadget, a last year's model."

"That's a harsh conclusion you make, Ves."

"But it's a true conclusion," Ves said with overwhelming intensity. "I've become a functionary, not a priestly apostle. When the mechanism no longer needed my functioning, it belched me out. And it's my own fault for not seeing where I was going, what I was doing, what I had made of myself. But now I see it." Then turning directly to Tom, with the same deep emotion, he blurted out, "Tom, its the finest sign of friendship that you helped me see it. It would have been easy to say nothing. But you've spoken out, and I'm grateful." Ves stopped abruptly, exhausted.

They sat in silence a while.

Finally Ves said: "I should be going."

"Before you push on, Ves," Tom suggested, "why don't we celebrate one last Mass that God will guide and protect you in whatever you do."

"That's a new thought, Tom, but you know I've never said Mass with another priest, except as deacon at High Mass. In fact, I've never said Mass in English. Further, I haven't offered Mass since I have been at Southwestern, because the Bishop said I either had to work with the people at the Newman Center or I couldn't function. So I haven't 'functioned.' I still read my breviary in Latin every day, abstain on Friday, and go to Mass every Sunday," and then as an after thought, "in a little out of the way church where they don't have a lot of guitars and hoopla."

"Okay, Ves. We won't have any guitars. We won't have any hoopla. And if you're willing to make a concession to newness, I'll make a concession to oldness. I don't believe, really, that we should offer private masses. I

152

believe so strongly that the mass is an act of social worship, that there always ought to be a congregation there. But I guess this time there really is a congregation."

"You'll have to tell me what to do."

"It's all on the card, Ves. You read the Epistle; I'll read the Gospel. Then we recite the prayers of the Consecration together. We'll use the second canon -- the shorter one."

"It's been such a long time, Tom, you better hear my confession."

"Okay, what's on your mind?"

"Well, my faith hasn't been too strong in the past few months. And while I have never missed Mass, I've been away from the Sacraments and I haven't gone to confession. I've thought some pretty uncharitable thoughts about the Superior and about the Roman Curia; not about the Pope, I just feel sorry for him. He has an impossible task. And I get so mad at these new fangled people with all their new-fangled ideas." He paused, stroked his clean-shaven chin, and went on. "I have had the ordinary run of bad thoughts and was slow in getting rid of them on several occasions. A little cursing -- and that's about it."

"Say three Hail Marys," Tom said and gave absolution. "Let's go to the sacristy."

Several old people who came in early for their Saturday confessions sat in the rear of the Church. The two began the Mass. When they reached the time for the Prayer of the Faithful, Tom said, "We'll select at random some of the prayers of the Office of the day." He opened his book to the first prayer he found; it was page 161 of his breviary. "By His Blood, Our Savior has made us a kingdom of priests to offer spiritual sacrifices acceptable to God. Let our prayer be."

"Keep us faithful to your service, Lord."

"Lord, may our life today be enlightened by our faith, may we proclaim this faith in our love and in all we do."

"Keep us faithful to your service, Lord."

"May we try to be helpful to everyone at all times; may our efforts work toward salvation."

"Keep us faithful to your service, Lord."

"You picked a telling prayer," Ves whispered.

"Please God, Ves. I didn't pick it. The book just opened to that page."

They went on with the Mass together. At its end, Tom gave the blessing: "Go in peace to love and serve the Lord."

153

"Thanks be to God," Ves responded.

A few minutes later, the two walked out to Ves' car. "Thanks, Tom," he said. "Pray for me."

He got into his car and drove back down Highway 3. As he passed the Chester Bridge and rode along the Mississippi he reflected on the prayers of the Mass and all the things Tom Meath had said. "Now I see it," he finally admitted to himself. "I've been a functionary, not an apostle!"

He stopped the car on the side of the road. He took the envelope from Rome out of his pocket. He tore the letter into small bits and threw the pieces into the Mississippi, and watched them float with the current. He moved the car back onto the highway.

Route 3 had turned away from the river, and as he approached Grimsby, he veered to the left on Highway 13. The sky had become more menacing. Rain seemed imminent. When he reached the Murphysboro Square, rain began to pound the windshield. He drove slowly through the eastern section of town because traffic was slow and the rain now came in waves. The windshield wipers sloshed back and forth in a vain effort to provide visibility. He reached the east end of town. The local traffic disappeared, but a few cars still moved ahead of him. Others turned off the road and stopped.

Ves continued on, presuming that it was as safe to move ahead slowly through the storm, as to stand and wait until it had swept by. He wondered how severe it would be. He saw no lightning. Suddenly he came to the end of the rain. Momentarily he congratulated himself for having kept going. But an eerie feeling filled the air, an amazing quiet, suggestive of trouble. He held down his fear as he suddenly realized that no other car moved on Highway 13.

At that moment, the sky turned a dread black. The wind whipped in fury. The rain came again, driving, as if from all directions. Ves flipped his windshield wiper back on. As he did, he could barely make out a culvert ahead. At that moment, the funnel cloud hit...

"This is Dan Pana reporting the 3:55 news over Station WRTH in Wood River. A funnel cloud struck down in the vicinity of Murphysboro and Carbondale, Illinois, shortly after three this afternoon. Property damages may reach over a million dollars, and there is one known dead. The dead man is Father Sylvester Baden, a priest of the Congregation of John Carroll, and a member of the faculty of Southwestern University. Father Baden was driving east on Highway 13. As he approached a culvert, the tornado threw his car into the abutment. Presumably he was killed instantly."

"A Visit to Utah"
from The Missionary Catechist, June, 1951

A first visit to a monastery of the Cistercian (or Trappist) Monks is an unforgettable experience. Fathers McCaul and Cullen of St. Joseph's parish, Ogden, offered to drive to Huntsville, about fourteen miles east of the city through a pass in the Wasatch Range. The state highway is well marked with signs that say "Monastery Six Miles," "Monastery Four Miles," and finally a pointer that leads the traveller off the state highway and down a country road, most of which had been built by the Monks themselves.

The monastery is a quadrangle of large quonsets, surmounted by a Cross, situated at the lower end of a small, rich valley -- a spot that would certainly satisfy St. Bernard's love of seclusion. A few cars of other visitors were parked there, one from Wyoming, another from California and three or four from Utah. Above the door stood a statue of Our Lady and the words, Pax Intrantibus.

One of our party rang the bell of the guest house. We could hear people talking inside, but there was no "Johnny-on-the-spot" response to our ring. It was our first taste of the unhurried pace of the Cistercians to whom not minutes but eternity counts.

The door opened and there was a rapid exchange of welcome in an unknown tongue that I soon recognized as Gaelic. Brother Matthew, the gate-keeper, formerly occupied a similar position at Gethsemani, where he admitted Thomas Merton twice, first as a retreatant, and then as a candidate for the Order. Brother now has at hand a number of Merton's books which the visitor may purchase for his spiritual consolation.

Brother Matthew is one of the most memorable men I have ever met. He has the strong handsome face of a pioneer and in his eyes is a peace unknown to most men of his generation. Brother asked my companions about the spiritual welfare of the young people of St. Joseph's parish, and then, turning to me, of a student at Regis College who had made a retreat there a year before. He may have left the "world" long ago, but he certainly remembered it in his prayers.

A few minutes later, Brother Matthew took us across the quadrangle and into the monastery proper. Here we were presented to the Father Abbot and the Guest Master who conducts the many retreats that are given. While the Monks gathered in the Chapel in preparation for Vespers and Benediction the Father Guest Master showed us around the building. Through a large window he pointed out the cattle barns that had served as a living quarters during the first rugged Utah winter.

Everything about the monastery is plain, neat and usable. There are no superfluities, either in the dining hall, the dormitory or the "scriptorium." As he pointed to the shelves loaded with ancient and recent spiritual books, the Guest Master remarked with a laugh, "We don't have Time and the other magazines."

The equipment is predominantly home-made, and quite attractive, the long desks in the scriptorium, for instance, and the brown clay dishes in the dining hall. Only the microphone that carries the Monks' spiritual reading to the retreatants' dining hall upstairs smacks of the mechanical age in which we live.

Monks walked quietly by us, as we made our tour of the monastery. There was no hurry about them, no feeling of fanaticism, but quiet peace, as they moved toward the chapel. A postulant approached us, and signalled his Superior for permission to converse. To my surprise, he was a former student of mine, who was to receive his white cowl on Low Sunday. He had come to Huntsville some months before, without so much as a letter to the Abbot announcing his approach.

By this time the tour was nearing its conclusion. It ended in the loft of the chapel. Immediately I thought of Thomas Merton's remarks about Cistercian architecture -- plain, but beautiful. One hardly thought a quonset could be so attractive. Later, when the priest approached the altar for Benediction, his orange-trimmed cope startled me. The rich colors clashed with the simplicity of the chapel.

The Cistercians do not genuflect, but retain their medieval custom of a deep bow from the waist in reverence to the Blessed Sacrament. The white-robed choir monks took their places along the walls to the front of the Church, the lay brothers in brown habit knelt in the rear. The Vespers of Mother Church began. God was near.

Before me seventy-two men worshipped, the vast majority veterans of the fighting fronts in World War II, young men most of them, with a strong, straight look about them. No fanaticism was present, or torturing fears of the Hounds of Hell. In the faces of all was strength and peace. Only one

156

of the monks, a tall, young man, seemed a bit nervous and hasty in manner. As another visitor later remarked, "You got the feeling that sanctifying grace was all over the monastery."

Suddenly I remembered Thomas Merton's remark that time seemed to stand still as the monks chanted. One had no desire to move or be about other business. Normally in such a situation I would have recited part of my Office or my Rosary. At Holy Trinity there was no desire to do so.

Slowly the beautiful chant of Vespers drew to a close. Hyms were sung. The blessing given, and the ceremony was over...

As we drove back to Ogden, I could not but think, as Merton has often told us, that here is a powerhouse of prayer to be reckoned with. Statesmen and atomic scientists might not find for us ways of peace. But the prayer of these men, who have given up the world and every worldly happiness in order to worship God and save their souls, may yet save the world they have renounced.

Father Faherty holds what few others on earth have held --
rocks from the moon. As official historian, Father Faherty
had an intimate look at the Apollo mission.

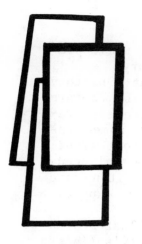

MOONPORT

John Kennedy told Congress in 1961 that "this nation should commit itself to achieving the goal, before this decade is out, of landing a man on the moon and returning him safely to earth." About this time Father Faherty, working with The Queen's Work in St. Louis, received the good news that Sheed and Ward had accepted Living Alone and that Academy Guild Press would publish A Wall for San Sebastian. The former has proved his best known book of priestly advice, the latter probably his best known work of fiction. Little did he know that work which would result in a widely read historical book had started with President Kennedy's pledge.

A decade later, he joined with Charles Benson to write the NASA History Series volume on the story of the Apollo space program. Working in Florida for two years, Barnaby Faherty took on the task of writing history immediately after it happened. This kind of task presents dangerous obstacles for the historian who finds himself selecting events, balancing interpretations, and evaluating data without the perspective that the passage of years brings. Further complicating his task, he had to rely on NASA - certainly an interested party -- for much of the information in the work. If these problems didn't suffice, there was the final difficulty of not slighting the

159

highly technical aspects of the project while producing an interesting and readable history.

Most able historians could present a history
of such a project; many novelists could capture
the drama inherent in a decade of space exploration. After all, many observers have named the
landing of humans on the moon as the most significant moment of the century. But a balanced,
thoroughly researched and reported, exciting and
sound history probably exceeded NASA's expectations.

We believe Chapter 18, "The Fire That Seared
the Spaceport," stands as Barnaby Faherty's finest
accomplishment. He achieves a surprising degree
of warmth by focusing on the people involved.
Characters like Tom "Discrepancy Report" Baron and
Dr. Kurt Debus emerge to appear as significant as
the actual program. The chapter -- as the book -
abounds in people. Likely, though, what accounts
for the brilliance of the chapter is the cool
careful description of the events preceding and
following the fire along with the account of the
fire itself. The surface of the prose moves un-
ruffled through the tragedy, while the subject
rumbles and quakes. The resulting understatement
and tension make this tale one of the best in
American writing.

"The Fire That Seared the Spaceport"
from Moonport

The thirteenth Saturn flight (the third Saturn IB) on
25 August 1966 was the thirteenth success. It fulfilled all
major mission objectives. For the first manned mission NASA
had selected two veterans and one rookie. Command Pilot
Virgil Ivan Grissom had flown Mercury's Liberty Bell 7,
America's second suborbital flight, in July 1961, and Molly
Brown, the first manned Gemini, in March 1965. Edward White
had become the first American to walk in space while on the
fourth Gemini flight, three months later. Flying with these
two would be the youngest American ever chosen to go into
space, Roger B. Chaffee, 31 years of age.

NASA gave Grissom the option of an open-ended mission.
The astronauts could stay in orbit up to 14 days, depending
on how well things went. The purpose of their flight was to

check out the launch operations, ground tracking and control facilities, and the performance of the Apollo-Saturn.

North American Aviation constructed the Apollo command and service modules. The spacecraft, 11 meters long and weighing about 27 metric tons when fully fueled, was considerably larger and more sophisticated than earlier space vehicles, with a maze of controls, gauges, dials, switches, lights, and toggles above the couches. Unlike the outward-opening hatches of the McDonnell-built spacecraft for Mercury and Gemini flights, the Apollo hatches opened inward. They required a minimum of ninety seconds for opening under routine conditions.

Many men, including Grissom, had presumed that serious accidents would occur in the testing of new spacecraft. A variety of things could go wrong. But most who admitted in the back of their minds that accidents might occur, expected them somewhere off in space.

Some individuals had misgivings about particular aspects of the spacecraft. Dr. Emmanuel Roth of the Lovelace Foundation for Medical Education and Research, for instance, prepared for NASA in 1964 a four-part series on "The Selection of Space-Cabin Atmospheres." He surveyed and summarized all the literature available at the time. He warned that combustible items, including natural fabrics and most synthetics, would burn violently in the pure oxygen atmosphere of the command module. Even allegedly flame-proof materials would burn. He warned against the use of combustibles in the vehicle.

In 1964 Dr. Frank J. Hendel, a staff scientist with Apollo Space Sciences and Systems at North American and the author of numerous articles and a textbook, contributed an article on "Gaseous Environment during Space Missions" to the Journal of Spacecraft and Rockets, a publication of the American Institute of Aeronautics and Astronautics. "Pure oxygen at five pounds per square inch of pressure," he wrote, "presents a fire hazard which is especially great on the launching pad....Even a small fire creates toxic products of combustion; no fire-fighting methods have yet been developed that can cope with a fire in pure oxygen."

Further, oxygen fires had occurred often enough to give safety experts cause for extra-careful procedures: at Brooks Air Force Base and at the Navy's Equipment Diving Unit at Washington, D.C., in 1965; and at the Airesearch Facility in Torrance, California, in 1964, 1965, and 1966.

One man saw danger on earth, from hazards other than fire. In November 1965, the American Society for Testing

and Materials held a symposium in Seattle on the operation
of manned space chambers. The papers gave great attention
to the length of time spent in the chambers, to decompres-
sion problems, and to safety programs. The Society published the proceedings under the title of Factors in the Operation of Manned Space Chambers (Philadelphia, 1966). In
reviewing this publication, Ronald G. Newswald concluded:
"With reliability figures and flight schedules as they are,
the odds are that the first casualty in space will occur on
the ground."

Since Newswald was a contributing editor of Space/Aero-
nautics, it may well be that he contributed the section entitled, "Men in Space Chambers: Guidelines Are Missing" in
the "Aerospace Perspective" section of that magazine during
the same month that his review appeared in Science Journal.
The editorial reflects the ideas and the wording of his review. The "Guidelines" writer began: "The odds are that
the first spaceflight casualty due to environmental exposure
will occur not in space, but on the ground." He saw no real
formulation of scientific procedures involving safety --
such as automatic termination of a chamber run in the event
of abnormal conditions. "By now," he stated, "NASA and
other involved agencies are well aware that a regularly up-
dated, progressive set of recommended practices -- engineering, medical and procedural -- for repressurization schedules and atmospheres, medical monitoring, safety rescue and
so on, would be welcome in the community."

Gen. Samuel Phillips, Apollo Program Director, had misgivings about the performance of North American Aviation,
the builder of the spacecraft, as early as the fall of 1965.
He had taken a task force to Downey, California, to go over
the management of the Saturn-II stage and command-service
module programs. The task force included Marshall's Eber-
hard Rees and the Apollo Spacecraft Program Manager, Joseph
Shea; they had many discussions with the officials of North
American. On 19 December 1965, Phillips wrote to John
Leland Atwood, the President of North American Aviation, en-
closing a "NASA Review Team Report," which later came to be
called the "Phillips Report." The visit of the task force
was not an unusual NASA procedure, but the analysis was more
intensive than earlier ones.

In the introduction, the purpose was clearly stated:
"The Review was conducted as a result of the continual failure of NAA to achieve the progress required to support the
objective of the Apollo program." The review included an
examination of the corporate organization and its relation-

ship to the Space Division, which was responsible for both the S-II stage and the command-service module, and an examination of North American Aviation's activities at Kennedy Space Center and the Mississippi Test Facility. The former area belongs more properly to the relations of North American Aviation with NASA Headquarters, but the latter directly affected activities at Kennedy Space Center.

Despite the elimination of some troublesome components and escalations in costs, both the S-11 stage and the spacecraft were behind schedule. The team found serious technical difficulties remaining with the insulation and welding on stage II and in stress corrosion and failure of oxidizer tanks on the command-service module. The "Report" pointed out that NAA's inability to meet deadlines had caused rescheduling of the total Apollo program and, with reference to the command-service module, "there is little confidence that NAA will meet its schedule and performance commitments."

Phillips and his task force returned to Downey for a follow-up week in mid-April 1966. He did not amend the original conclusions, but he told President Atwood that North American was moving in the right direction.

The astronauts themselves suggested many changes in the block I spacecraft design. In April 1967, Donald K. Slayton was to tell the Subcommittee on NASA Oversight of the House Committee on Science and Astronautics that the astronauts had recommended 45 improvements, including a new hatch. North American had acted on 39 of these recommendations. They were introducing the other six into later spacecraft. "Most of these," Slayton testified, "were of a relatively minor nature." The only major change for later spacecraft was to have been a new hatch. And the astronauts had recommended this not so much for safety as for ease in getting out for space-walks and at the end of flights.

In July and August 1966, NASA officials conducted a customer acceptance readiness review at North American Aviation's Downey plant, issued a certificate of worthiness, and authorized spacecraft 012 to be shipped to the Kennedy Space Center. The certificate listed incomplete work: North American Aviation had not finished 113 significant engineering orders at the time of delivery.

The command module arrived at KSC on 26 August and went to the pyrotechnic installation building for a weight and balance demonstration. With the completion of the thrust vector alignment on 29 August, the test team moved the command module to the altitude chamber in the operations and checkout building and began mating the command and service modules. Minor problems with the service module had already showed up, and considerable difficulties with the new mating hardware caused delays.

On 7 September NASA released a checkout schedule. By 14 September, while the Saturn launch vehicle moved on schedule, the Apollo spacecraft already lagged four days behind. On the same day, a combined systems test was begun. Discrepancy reports numbered 80 on 16 September and had risen to 152 within sixty days. One of the major problems was a short in the radio command system. In the meantime, the first team had installed all but one of the flight panels.

At Headquarters during this time, a board chaired by the Associate Administrator for Manned Space Flight, Dr. George Mueller, and made up of OMSF center directors, conducted a detailed review of the spacecraft. On 7 October this board certified the design as "flightworthy, pending satisfactory resolution of listed open items."

The simulated altitude run, originally scheduled for 26 September, had gradually slipped back in schedule. It was run on 11 October, but plans for an unmanned altitude run on 12 October, a flight crew altitude run on 14 October, and a backup crew run on 15 October also slipped. So did the projected dates of mechanical mating of the spacecraft with the launch vehicle and the launch itself.

The unmanned altitude chamber run finished satisfactorily on 15 October. The first manned run in the altitude test chamber, on 18 October, experienced trouble after reaching a simulated altitude of 4000 meters because of the failure of a transistor in one of the inverters. With the replacement of the inverter, the system functioned satisfactorily. The prime crew of Grissom, White, and Chaffee repeated the 16-hour run the next day with only one major problem developing in the oxygen cabin supply regulator. This problem caused a delay of the second manned run with the backup crew scheduled for 21 October. Continued trouble with the new oxygen regulator caused the indefinite suspension of the second manned test before the end of October. By this time it had become clear that the spacecraft needed a new environmental control unit. Technicians removed the old unit on 1 November.

Meanwhile, at North American Aviation's Downey plant a propellant tank had ruptured in the service module of spacecraft 017. This provoked a special test of the propellant tanks on the 012 service module at KSC. In order to conduct this testing in parallel with further checking of the command module, the test team removed the command module from the altitude chamber. Later they removed the fuel tanks from the service module in the chamber. After pressure-integrity tests, they replaced the tanks and returned the command module to the chamber. The test team installed and fit-checked the new environmental control unit on 8 November and hooked up the interface lines two days later. But this did not completely solve the difficulties. Problems in the glycol cooling system surfaced toward the end of November and on 5 December forced a removal of the second environmental control unit.

The Apollo Review Board was to say of this glycol leakage several months later,

> water/glycol coming into contact with electrical connectors can cause corrosion of these connectors. Dried water/glycol on wiring insulation leaves a residue which is electrically conductive and combustible. Of the six recorded instances where water/glycol spillage or leakage occurred (a total of 90 ounces leaked or spilled is noted in the records) the records indicate that this resulted in wetting of conductors and wiring on only one occasion. There is no evidence which indicates that damage resulted to the conductors or that faults were produced on connectors due to water/glycol.

The difficulties in the materials that already had arrived at KSC and the endless changes that came in from North American Aviation -- 623 distinct engineering orders -- presented major problems for the NASA-NAA test teams. As many workmen as could possibly function inside the command module continually swarmed into it to replace defective equipment or make the changes that NAA suggested and Houston approved. The astronauts came and went, sometimes concerned with major and sometimes with minor matters on the spacecraft.

These difficulties at KSC and concurrent problems at Mission Control Center, Houston, forced two revisions to the schedule, one on 17 November, the next on 9 December. The test team kept up with or moved ahead of the latter schedule during the ensuing weeks. The third environmental control unit arrived for installation on 16 December.

The test teams had been working on a 24-hour basis since the arrival of the spacecraft at Kennedy, taking off only Christmas and New Year's Day. On 28 December, while conducting an unmanned altitude run, the test team located a radio frequency communications problem and referred it to ground support technicians for correction. On 30 December a new backup crew of Schirra, Eisele, and Cunningham (McDivitt's original backup crew had received a new assignment) successfully completed a manned altitude run. Six major problems on the spacecraft surfaced, one in very-high-frequency radio communications; but a review board was to give a favorable appraisal not long afterward: "This final manned test in the altitude chamber was very successful with all spacecraft systems functioning normally. At the post-test debriefing the backup flight crew expressed their satisfaction with the condition and performance of the spacecraft."

By 5 January the mating of the spacecraft to the lunar module adapter and the ordnance installation were proceeding six days ahead of schedule. The following day the space craft was moved from the operations and checkout building to LC-34. KSC advanced the electrical mating and the emergency detection system tests to 18 January, and these were completed that day. The daily status report for 20 January 1967 reported that no significant problems occurred during the plugs-in overall test. A repeat of the test on 25 January took 24 hours. A problem in the automatic checkout equipment link-up caused the delay. Further, the instrument unit did not record simulated liftoff -- a duplication of an earlier deficiency. The schedule called for a plugs-in test at 3:00 p.m. on 26 January, a test in which the vehicle would rely on internal power. NASA did not rate the plugs-in test as "hazardous," reserving that label for tests involving fueled vehicles, hypergolic propellants, cryogenic systems, high-pressure tanks, live pyrotechnics, or altitude chamber tests.

All the tests and modifications in the spacecraft did not go far enough or fast enough in the view of one North American employee, Thomas R. Baron of Mims, Florida. Baron's story has significance for two reasons. His attitude reflected the unidentified worries of many who did not express them until too late. Also, the reaction of KSC managers indicated a determination to check every lead that might uncover an unsafe condition. The local press at the time gave ample but one-sided coverage of the Baron story.

Baron had a premonition of disaster. He believed his company would not respond to his warnings and wanted to get his message to the top command at KSC. While a patient at

Jeff Parish Hospital in Titusville, Florida, during December, 1966, and later at Holiday Hospital in Orlando, Baron expressed his fears to a number of people. His roommate at Jeff Parish happened to be a KSC technical writer, Michael Mogilevsky. After Baron claimed to have in his possession documentary evidence of deficiencies in the heat shield, cabling, and life support systems, Mogilevsky went to see Frank Childers in NASA Quality Control on 16 December. Childers called in an engineer of the Office of the Director of Quality Assurance, and Mogilevsky related Baron's complaints and fears again.

That evening Rocco Petrone asked John M. Brooks, the Chief of NASA's Regional Inspections Office, to locate and interview Baron. Brooks interviewed Baron twice and briefed Debus, Albert Siepert, and Petrone on Baron's complaints: poor workmanship, failure to maintain cleanliness, faulty installation of equipment, improper testing, unauthorized deviations from specifications and instructions, disregard for rules and regulations, lack of communication between Quality Control and engineering organizations and personnel, and poor personnel practices.

Baron claimed to possess notebooks that would substantiate his charges. He promised to cooperate with KSC and with North American Aviation if someone above his immediate supervisor would listen to what he had to say. He did not believe his previous complaints had ever gone beyond that supervisor. He asked to be allowed to talk to John Hansel, Chief of Quality Control for North American. Baron's complaints were against North American, not KSC. He believed that the center needed additional personnel to enforce compliance with procedures in the Apollo program. Brooks later reported: "Baron was assured that an appropriate level of NAA management would be in touch with him in the next day or two."

On 22 December 1966, Petrone and Wiley E. Williams, Test and Operations Management Office, Directorate for Spacecraft Operations, received a briefing on Baron's complaints. The two men recognized that these were primarily North American Aviation in-house problems and that the company should inquire into Baron's complaints and advise KSC officials of the results. NAA officials W.S. Ford, James L. Pearce, and John L. Hansel met with Petrone that same day. They arranged to talk with Baron the following day.

Since Baron had confidence in Hansel, who was an expert in Quality Control, Hansel's testimony is especially valuable. Baron had lots of complaints but, Hansel insisted, no real proof of major deficiencies, either in the papers Baron had in his possession or in the report that Baron wrote (and Hansel was to read) a short time later. Lastly, Hansel stated, Baron was not working in a critical area at that time.

North American informed Petrone of the interview by 4 January, but sent no written report to Petrone's office. On 5 January a North American spokesman told newsmen that the company was terminating Baron's services. Since his clearance at the space center had been withdrawn, Baron phoned John Brooks, the NASA inspector, on 24 January and invited him to his home. Brooks accepted the invitation, and Baron gave him a 57-page report for duplication and use. Brooks duplicated it and returned the original to Baron on 25 January. Brooks assured Baron that KSC and NAA had looked into his allegations and taken corrective action where necessary.

Petrone received a mimeographed copy of Baron's report on 26 January. John Wasik of the Titusville Star Advocate telephoned Brooks to ask about KSC's interest in Baron's information. Wasik indicated that he was going to seek an interview with Petrone. On the following morning, Gordon Harris, head of the Public Affairs Office at KSC, heard that Wasik had spent approximately one and one-half hours with Zack Strickland, of the North American Aviation Public Relations Information Office, going over the Baron report.

That same day Hansel, North American's head of Quality Control -- the man Baron had hoped his report would reach -- told Wasik that Baron was one of the most conscientious quality control men he ever had working for him and that his work was always good. "If anything," Hansel related in the presence of Strickland, "Baron was too much of a perfectionist. He couldn't bend and allow deviations from test procedures -- and anyone knows that when you're working in a field like this, there is constant change and improvement. The test procedures written in an office often don't fit when they are acutally applied. Baron couldn't understand this." Wasik also stated: "Hansel readily agreed that Baron's alleged discrepancies were, for the most part, true." What Wasik did not say was that none of the discrepancies, true though they were, were serious enough to cause a disaster.

Hansel was not alone in his misgivings about Baron. Hansel did not know of Frank Childers's report nor had he ever talked to Childers about Baron. Childers, too, had doubts about the man's reliability. Even though he had sympathetically reported to NASA officials the fears of the

North American employee, Childers admitted that Baron, who signed himself T.R. Baron, had the nickname "D.R. (Discrepancy Report) Baron." R.E. Reyes, an engineer in KSC's Preflight Operations Branch, said Baron filed so many negative charges that, had KSC heeded them all, NASA would not have had a man on the moon until the year 2069. To confirm the opinions of these men, Baron himself admitted before a congressional investigating committee a short time later that he had turned in so many negative reports that his department ran out of the proper forms. Further -- in confirmation of Hansel's view of Baron's report -- Baron based his testimony on hearsay, not on any personal records in his possession. Baron's forebodings were to prove correct, but not for any reason he could document.

Both NASA and North American Aviation, a historian must conclude, gave far more serious consideration to Baron's complaints than a casual perusal of newspapers during the succeeding weeks, or even close reading of such books as Mission to the Moon, would indicate.

While top administrators were checking out the fears of Tom Baron, two NASA men, Clarence Chauvin and R.E. Reyes, and two North American Project Engineers, Bruce Haight and Chuck Hannon, met on the morning of 26 January at launch complex 34 to review the general spacecraft readiness and configuration for one of the last major previews, the plugs-out test. The craft looked ready.

That same night the prime and backup crews studied mission plans. The next day a simulated countdown would start shortly before liftoff and then the test would carry through several hours of flight time. There would be no fuel in the Saturn. Grissom, White, and Chaffee would don their full spacesuits and enter the Apollo, breathing pure oxygen to approximate orbital conditions as closely as possible. After simulated liftoff, the spacecraft center in Houston would monitor the performance of the astronauts. The plugs-out test did not rate a hazardous classification; the spacecraft had successfully operated in the test chamber for a greater period of time than it would on the pad.

The astronauts entered the Apollo at 1:00 p.m., Friday, 27 January 1967. Problems immediately arose. NASA Spacecraft Test Conductor Clarence Chauvin later described them: "The first problem that we encountered was when Gus Grissom ingressed into the spacecraft and hooked up to his oxygen supply from the spacecraft. Essentially, his first words were that there was a strange odor in the suit loop. He described it as a 'sour smell' somewhat like buttermilk."

A PRIEST FOR ALL REASON

The crew stopped to take a sample of the suit loop, and after discussion with Grissom decided to continue the test.

The next problem was a high oxygen flow indication which periodically triggered the master alarm. The men discussed this matter with environmental control systems personnel, who believed the high flow resulted from movements of the crew. The matter was not really resolved.

A third serious problem arose in communications. At first, faulty communications seemed to exist solely between Command Pilot Grissom and the control room. The crew made adjustments. Later, the difficulty extended to include communications between the operations and checkout building and the blockhouse at complex 34. "The overall communications problem was so bad at times," Chauvin testified, "that we could not even understand what the crew was saying." William H. Schick, Assistant Test Supervisor in the blockhouse at complex 34, reported in at 4:30 p.m. and monitored the spacecraft checkout procedure for the Deputy of Launch Operations. He sat at the test supervisor's console and logged the events, including various problems in communications. To complicate matters further, no one person controlled the trouble-shooting of the communications problem. This failure in communication forced a hold of the countdown at 5:40 p.m. By 6:31 the test conductors were about ready to pick up the count when ground instruments showed an unexplained rise in the oxygen flow into the spacesuits. One of the crew, presumably Grissom moved slightly.

Four seconds later, an astronuat, probably Chaffee, announced almost causally over the intercom: "Fire, I smell fire." Two seconds later, Astronaut White's voice was more insistent: "Fire in the cockpit."

In the blockhouse, engineers and technicians looked up from their consoles to the television monitors trained at the spacecraft. To their horror, they saw flames licking furiously inside Apollo, and smoke blurred their pictures. Men who had gone through Mercury and Gemini tests and launches without a major hitch stood momentarily stunned at the turn of events. Their eyes saw what was happening, but their minds refused to believe. Finally a near hysterical shout filled the air: "There's a fire in the spacecraft!"

Procedures for emergency escape called for a minimum of 90 seconds. But in practice the crew had never accomplished the routines in the minimum time. Grissom had to lower White's headrest so White could reach above and behind his left shoulder to actuate a ratchet-type device that would release the first series of latches. According to one source, White had actually made part of a full turn with the ratchet before he was overcome by smoke. In the meantime, Chaffee had carried out his duties by switching the power and then turning up the cabin lights as an aid to vision. Outside the white room that totally surrounded the spacecraft, Donald O. Babbitt of North American Aviation ordered emergency procedures to rescue the astronauts. Technicians started toward the white room. Then the command module ruptured.

Wittnesses differed as to how fast everything happened. Gary W. Propst, an RCA technician at the communication control racks in Area D on the first floor at launch complex 34, testified four days later that three minutes elapsed between the first shout of "Fire" and the filling of the white room with smoke. Other observers had gathered around his monitor and discussed why the astronauts did not blow the hatch and why no one entered the white room. One of these men, A. R. Caswell, testified on 2 February, two days after Propst. In answer to a question about the time between the first sign of fire and activity outside the spacecraft in the white room, he said: "It appeared to be quite a long period of time, perhaps three or four minutes..."

The men on the launch tower told a different story. Bruce W. Davis, a systems technician with North American Aviation who was on level A8 of the service structure at the time of the fire, reported an almost instantaneous spread of fire from the moment of first warning. "I heard someone say, 'There is a fire in the cockpit.' I turned around and after about one second I saw flames within the two open access panels in the command module near the umbilical." Jessie L. Owens, North American Systems Engineer, stood near the pad leader's desk when someone shouted: "Fire." He heard what sounded like the cabin relief valve opening and high velocity gas escaping. "Immediately this gas burst into flames somewhat like lighting an acetylene torch," he said. "I turned to go to the white room at the above-noted instant, but was met by a flame wall."

Spacecraft technicians ran toward the sealed Apollo, but before they could reach it, the command module ruptured. Flame and thick black clouds of smoke billowed out, filling the room. Now a new danger arose. Many feared that the fire might set off the launch escape system atop Apollo. This, in turn, could ignite the entire service structure. Instinct told the men to get out while they could. Many did so, but others tried to rescue the astronauts.

Approximately 90 seconds after the first report of

fire, pad leader Donald Babbitt reported over a headset from the swing arm that his men had begun attempts to open the hatch. Thus the panel that investigated the fire concluded that only one minute elapsed between the first warning of the fire and the rescue attempt. Babbitt's personal recollection of his reporting over the headset did not make it clear that he had already been in the white room, as the panel seemed to conclude. Be that as it may, for more than five minutes, Babbitt and his North American Aviation crew of James D. Gleaves, Jerry W. Hawkins, Steven B. Clemmons, and L.D. Reece, and NASA's Henry H. Rodgers, Jr., struggled to open the hatch. The intense heat and dense smoke drove one after another back, but finally they succeeded. Unfortunately, it was too late. The astronauts were dead. Firemen arrived within three minutes of the hatch opening, doctors soon thereafter. A medical board was to determine that the astronauts died of carbon monoxide asphyxsia, with thermal burns as contributing causes. The board could not say how much of the burns came after the three had died. Fire had destroyed 70% of Grissom's spacesuit, 25% of White's, and 15% of Chaffee's. Doctors treated 27 men for smoke inhalation. Two were hospitalized.

Rumors of disaster spread in driblets through the area. Men who had worked on the day shift returned to see if they could be of help. Crewmen removed the three charred bodies well after midnight.

The sudden deaths of the three astronauts caused international grief and widespread questioning of the space program. Momentarily the whole manned lunar program stood in suspense. Writing in Newsweek, Walter Lippman immediately deplored what he called the pride-spurred rush of the program. The Washington Sunday Star spoke of soaring costs and claimed that "know-who" had more to do than "know-how" in the choice of North American over Martin Marietta as prime contractor for the spacecraft. A long-time critic of the space program, Senator William J. Fulbright of Arkansas, Chairman of the Senate Foreign Relations Committee, placed the "root cause of the tragedy" in "the inflexible, but meaningless, goal of putting an American on the moon by 1970" and called for a "full reappraisal of the space program." The distinguished scientist Dr. James A. Van Allen, discoverer of radiation belts in space, charged that NASA was "losing its soul." It had become "a huge engineering, technological and operational agency with less and less devotion to the true spirit of exploration and to the advancement of basic knowledge." A lead editorial in the New York

Times spoke of the incompetence and negligence that became apparent as the full story of disaster came to light, but put the central blame on "the technically senseless" and "highly dangerous" dedication to the meaningless timetable of putting a man on the moon by 1970. An article in the American Institute of Chemical Engineers Journal had the long-anticipated title: "NASA's in the Cold, Cold Ground." But President Johnson held firm to the predetermined goal and communicated his confidence to NASA.

After removal of the bodies, NASA impounded everything at launch complex 34. On 3 February, NASA Administrator Webb set up a review board to investigate the matter thoroughly. Except for one Air Force officer and an explosives expert from the Bureau of Mines, both specialists in safety, all the members of the board came from NASA. North American Aviation had a man on the board for one day. At least George Jeffs, NAA's chief Apollo engineer, thought he was on the board. After consultation with Shea and Gilruth of the Manned Space Flight Center, North American officials recommended him as one who could contribute more than any other NAA officer. Jeffs sat in on several meetings at KSC, until, as he was to report later to the House Subcommittee on NASA Oversight, "I was told that I was no longer a member of the Board." The representative of the review board who dismissed Jeffs gave no reason for the dismissal. Thus all members of the board were government employees, a fact that was to cause NASA considerable criticism from Congress.

Debus asked all KSC and contractor employees for complete cooperation with the review board. He called their attention to the Apollo Mission Failure Contingency Plan of 13 May 1966 that prohibited all government and contractor employees from discussing technical aspects of the accident with anyone other than a member of the board. All press information would go through the Public Affairs Office. In scheduled public addresses, speakers might discuss other aspects of the space program but "should courteously but absolutely refuse to speculate at this time on anything connected with the Apollo 204 investigation or with factors that might be related, directly or indirectly, to the accident." Debus's action muted at KSC the wild rumors that had prevailed in east Florida and spread throughout the country after the fire.

Under authorization from the review board, ground crews carefully removed the debris on the crew couches inside the command module on 3 February. They recorded the type and location of the material removed. Then they laid a plywood

173

shelf across the three interlocked seats so that combustion specialists could enter the command module and examine the cabin more thoroughly. On the following day they removed the plywood and the three seats. Two days after that, they suspended a plastic false floor inside the command module so that investigators could continue to examine the command module interior without aggravating the condition of the lower part of the cabin.

Engineers at the Manned Spacecraft Center duplicated conditions of Apollo 204 without crewmen in the capsule. They reconstructed events as studies at KSC brought them to light. The investigation on pad 34 showed that the fire started in or near one of the wire bundles to the left and just in front of Grissom's seat on the left side of the cabin -- a spot visible to Chaffee. The fire was probably invisible for about five or six seconds until Chaffee sounded the alarm. "From then on," a Time writer stated, "the pattern and the intensity of the test fire followed, almost to a second, the pattern and intensity of the fire aboard Apollo 204."

The members of the review board sifted every ash in the command module, photographed every angle, checked every wire, and questioned in exhausting detail almost everyone who had the remotest knowledge of events related to the fire. They carefully dismantled and inspected every component in the cockpit.

In submitting its formal report to Administrator Webb on 5 April 1967, the board summarized its findings: "The fire in Apollo 204 was most probably brought about by some minor malfunction or failure of equipment or wire insulation. This failure, which most likely will never be positively identified, initiated a sequence of events that culminated in the conflagration.

To the KSC Safety Office, the next finding of the Review Board seemed to be the key to the entire report: "Those organizations responsible for the planning, conduct and safety of this test failed to identify it as being hazzardous." Since NASA had not considered the test hazardous, KSC had not instituted those procedures that normally would have accompanied such a test.

> The Review Board had other severe criticism:
> Deficiencies existed in Command Module design, workmanship and quality control...
> The Command Module contained many types
> and classes of combustible material in areas

contiguous to possible ignition sources...The
rapid spread of fire caused an increase in pressure and temperature which resulted in rupture of
the Command Module and creation of a toxic atmosphere...Due to internal pressure, the Command
Module inner hatch could not be opened prior to
rupture of Command Module...The overall communications system was unsatisfactory...Problems of
program management and relationships between
Centers and with the contractor have led in some
cases to insufficient response to changing program
requirements...Emergency fire, rescue and medical
teams were not in attendance...The Command Module
Environmental Control System design provides a
pure oxygen atmosphere...This atmosphere presents
severe fire hazards.

A last recommendation went beyond hazards: "Every effort must be made to insure the maximum clarification and
understanding of the responsibilities of all the organizations involved, the objective being a fully coordinated and
efficient program."
The review board recommended that NASA continue its
program and get to the moon and back before the end of 1969.
Safety, however, was to be a prime consideration, outranking
the target date. The board urged, finally, that NASA keep
the appropriate congressional committees informed on significant problems arising in its programs.
Astronaut Frank Borman, a member of the board, summed
up the fact that everyone had taken safety in ground testing
for granted. The crewmen, he stated, had the right not to
enter the spacecraft if they thought it was unsafe. However, "none of us," Borman insisted, "gave any serious consideration to a fire in the spacecraft."
The board members sharply criticized the fact that the
astronauts had no quick means of escape and recommended a
redesigned hatch that could be opened in two or three seconds instead of a minute and a half. They proposed a number
of other changes in the design of both the spacecraft and
the pad and recommended revised practices and procedures for
emergencies. Many of these, incidentally, KSC already had
in its plans for "hazardous" operations.
One of the most amazing facts to come out in the testimony of so many at KSC was the complicated process of communications. A contractor employee would confer with his
NASA counterpart, who would in turn get in touch with his

supervisor, who would in turn report to someone else in the chain of command. It must have seemed to the review board easier for a man on the pad to get through to the White House than to reach a local authority in time of an emergency.

When the review board began its investigation in February, the Senate Committee on Aeronautical and Space Sciences held a few hearings but confined its queries to major NASA officials. When the Apollo 204 Review Board turned in its report to Administrator Webb, the Senate Committee enlarged the scope of its survey; and the House Committee on Science and Astronautics, more particularly the Subcommittee on NASA Oversight, went into action.

Congress had wider concerns, however, than the mechanics of the fire that had occupied so much of the review board's time. Both houses, and especially two legislators from Illinois, freshman Senator Charles Percy and Representative Donald Rumsfeld, showed great interest in the composition of the review board, especially its lack of non-government investigators. Members of Congress questioned the board's omission of any analysis of the possibility of weakness in the managerial structure that might have allowed conditions to approach the point of disaster. Senator Edward Brooke of Massachusetts wondered about the extensive involvement of North American Aviation and its capacity to handle such a huge percentage of the Apollo contracts. To the surprise of both NASA and NAA officials, members of both the Senate and House committees were to take a growing interest in the report of the Phillips review team of December 1965. This probing was to lead to some embarrassing moments for Mueller of NASA and Atwood of North American Aviation. But these aspects of the hearings belong more properly to the NASA Headquarters history.

Questioning of Debus by two members of the House Committee on Science and Astronautics at a hearing in Washington on the evening of 12 April bears directly on the KSC story. Congressman John Wydler of New York asked Debus to clarify his secrecy directive, which Wydler believed had caused some misunderstanding. Debus read his initial directive of 3 February, which asked for total cooperation with the board and squelched other discussion of the disaster; and then his second announcement of 11 April, after the review board had submitted its report, which removed all restraints. Wydler seemed satisfied.

When Congressman James Fulton of Pennsylvania asked Debus a few minutes later if he would like to make a short statement for the record, Debus came out candidly:

> As director of the installation I share
> the responsibility for this tragic accident
> and I have given it much thought. It is for
> me very difficult to find out why we did not
> think deeply enough or were not inventive
> enough to identify this as a very hazardous
> test.
> I have searched in my past for safety
> criteria that we developed in the early days
> of guided missile work and I must say that
> there are some that are subject to intuitive
> thinking and forward assessment. Some are
> made by practical experience and involved not
> only astronauts but the hundreds of people on
> the pads...
> It is very deplorable but it was the
> known condition which started from Commander
> Shepard's flight...from then on we developed
> a tradition that...considered the possibility
> of a fire but we had no concept of the pos-
> sible viciousness of this fire and its speed.
> We never knew that the conflagration
> would go that fast through the spacecraft so
> that no rescue would essentially help. This
> was not known. This is the essential cause
> of the tragedy. Had we known, we would have
> prepared with as adequate support as humanly
> possible for egress.

Congressman Fulton congratulated Debus on his statement. "This is why we have confidence in NASA. We have
been with you on previous failures, not so tragic... The Air
Force had five consecutive failures and this committee still
backed them and said go ahead." By looking at matters
openly and seeking better procedures, Fulton felt that NASA
was making progress.

The House Subcommittee on NASA Oversight, under the
chairmanship of Olin Teague of Texas, held hearings at the
Kennedy Space Center on 21 April. When the investigation
opened, it soon became clear -- as the review board had already learned -- that any emergency procedures at the space
center would be extremely complicated matters involving conferences between NASA and contractor counterparts, and even

in certain instances with representatives of the Air Force safety section. Beyond this the most noteworthy event of the hearing was the recommendation of Congressman Daddario that the members commend the brave men on the pad who had tried to save the astronauts.

While the Senate committee in Washington spent a great deal of time on the Phillips report, and embarrassed NASA and NAA officials with questions about the document, the committee finally had to agree with the testimony that "the findings of the Phillips task force had no effect on the accident, did not lead to the accident, and were not related to the accident." On the positive side, the committee learned from President Atwood that North American Aviation had made substantial changes in its management. The firm had placed William B. Bergen, former president of Martin-Marietta, in charge of its Space Division; obtained the full-time services of Bastian Hello and hired as consultant G. T. Wiley, both former Martin officials; and transferred one of its own officers, P. R. Vogt, from the Rocketdyne Division to the Space Division. Atwood testified that North American would probably make other changes. In the end, the Senate committee recommended that NASA move forward to achieve its goal within the prescribed time, but reaffirmed the review board's insistence that safety take precedence over target dates, and reminded NASA to keep appropriate congressional committees informed of any significant problems that might arise in its program.

During the ensuing months, NASA took many steps to prevent future disasters. It gave top priority to a redesigned hatch, a single-hinged door that swung outward with only one-half pound of force. An astronaut could unlatch the door in three seconds. The hatch had a push-pull unlatching handle, a window for visibility in flight, a plunger handle inside the command module to unlatch a segment of the protective cover, a pull loop that permitted someone outside to unlatch the protective cover, and a counterbalance that would hold the door open. NASA revised flight schedules. An unmanned Saturn V would go up in late 1967, but the manned flight of the backup crew for the Grissom team -- Schirra, Eisele, and Cunningham -- would not be ready before the following May or June. In the choice of materials for space suits, NASA settled on a new flame-proof material called "Beta Cloth" instead of nylon. Within the spacecraft, technicians covered exposed wires and plumbing to preclude inadvertent contact, redesigned wire bundles and harness routings, and increased fire protection.

Initially, NASA administrators said they would stay with oxygen as the atmosphere in the spacecraft. But after a year and a half of testing, NASA was to settle on a formula of 60% oxygen and 40% nitrogen. NASA provided a spacecraft mockup at KSC for training the rescue and the operational teams. At complex 34 technicians put a fan in the white room to ventilate any possible smoke. They added water hoses and fire extinguishers and an escape slide wire. Astronauts and workers could ride down this wire during emergencies, reaching the ground from a height of over 60 meters in seconds.

NASA safety officers were instructed to report directly to the center director. At Kennedy this procedure had been the practice for some time. A Headquarters decision also extended the responsibilities of the Flight Safety Office at Kennedy. Test conductors and all others intimately involved with the development of the spacecraft and its performance sent every change in procedure to the Flight Safety Office for approval.

The fire had a significant impact on KSC's relations with the spacecraft contractors. When KSC had absorbed Houston's Florida Opeations team in December 1964, the launch center was supposed to have assumed direction of the spacecraft contractors at the Cape. The North American and Grumman teams at KSC, however, had continued to look to their home offices, and indirectly to Houston, for guidance. This ended in the aftermath of LC-34's tragedy. With the support of NASA Headquarters, KSC took firm control of all spacecraft activities at the launch center.

To strengthen program management further, NASA entered into a contract with the Boeing Company to assist and support the NASA Apollo organization in the performance of specific technical integration and evaluation functions. NASA retained responsibility for final technical decisions. This Boeing-TIE contract, as it came to be called at KSC, proved the most controversial of all post-fire precautions. Many in middle or lower echelons at KSC criticized it. They looked upon it as a public relations scheme to convince Congress of NASA's sincere effort to promote safety.

Even NASA Headquarters found it difficult to explain to a congressional subcommittee either the expenditure of $73 million in one year on the contract, or that it had hired a firm to inspect work which that firm itself performed. As a matter of fact one segment of the Boeing firm -- that working under the TIE contract -- had to check on another, the one that worked on the first stage of Saturn V. Mueller explained to the committee that "the Boeing selection for the TIE contract...was based upon the fact that this was an extension of the work [Boeing personnel] were already doing in terms of integrating the Saturn V launch vehicle."

ABOUT THE CO-AUTHORS

Angela Harris and Dick Friedrich have made the students of midwestern community colleges aware of their writing and teaching skills with two popular textbooks in English composition, WRITING FOR YOUR READER and VISIONS AND REVISIONS. As members of the faculty of Forest Park Community College, they write well, teach well, and know literature...

A native of Saint Louis, Angela attended Fontbonne College and completed her master's degree at the University of Kansas. After two years on the faculty of the University of Missouri-Saint Louis, she accepted a more challenging and rewarding post at Forest Park Community College.

She published articles on two contemporary literary figures, the poet Sister Madaleva and Renaissance scholar Walter Ong. Her article on literary landmarks of Saint Louis was reprinted by the Post Dispatch.

A fan of the Saint Louis Cardinals, both football and baseball, Angela confines her own athletic activities to jogging. She travels extensively in the Pacific Northwest, a favorite part of the country...

Dick Friedrich points with satisfaction to another book, this one co-authored with David Keuster, entitled IT'S MINE, AND I'LL WRITE IT THAT WAY. Dick has also published one play, "J.C.", in WIN Magazine. Audiences have seen the production in New York, Wisconsin and Arkansas.

A native of Chicago and a graduate of St. Procopius College in up-state Illinois, Dick did his graduate work at the University of Wisconsin-Madison and taught for nine years at UW- Stout. Dick rates composition his favorite college course; and he names Walt Whitman and Emily Dickinson his favorite American authors of the past century.

Photos by Bob Arteaga, Eldon Arteaga and Denny Silverstein.